DIGITAL
(R)EVOLUTION

DIGITAL
(R)EVOLUTION

Strategies to Accelerate Business Transformation

YURI AGUIAR

WILEY

Published by John Wiley & Sons, Inc., Hoboken, New Jersey.
Published simultaneously in Canada.

For general information on our other products and services or for technical support, please contact our Customer Care Department within the United States at (800) 762–2974, outside the United States at (317) 572–3993, or fax (317) 572–4002.

Wiley publishes in a variety of print and electronic formats and by print-on-demand. Some material included with standard print versions of this book may not be included in e-books or in print-on-demand. If this book refers to media such as a CD or DVD that is not included in the version you purchased, you may download this material at http://booksupport.wiley.com. For more information about Wiley products, visit www.wiley.com.

Library of Congress Cataloging-in-Publication Data:

Names: Aguiar, Yuri, author.
Title: Digital (r)evolution : strategies to accelerate business
    transformation / Yuri B Aguiar.
Description: First Edition. | Hoboken : Wiley, 2020. | Includes index.
Identifiers: LCCN 2019053582 (print) | LCCN 2019053583 (ebook) | ISBN
    9781119619734 (hardback) | ISBN 9781119619741 (adobe pdf) | ISBN
    9781119619789 (epub)
Subjects: LCSH: Business enterprises—Technological innovations. |
    Information technology—Management. | Strategic planning.
Classification: LCC HD45 .A4768 2020 (print) | LCC HD45 (ebook) | DDC
    658.4/06—dc23
LC record available at https://lccn.loc.gov/2019053582
LC ebook record available at https://lccn.loc.gov/2019053583

Cover Design: Wiley/Aaron Aguiar
Cover Image: © imaginima/Getty Images

Printed in the United States of America

V10018216_032520

For Lynn, who taught me resilience

*For Aaron and Brandon, who inspire
me every day*

*For my parents, who taught me the
value of hard work*

*For my grandmother, my role model
growing up*

*For family and friends who were always
there through the good times
and otherwise*

CONTENTS

FOREWORD

Waterwheels transformed agriculture and electricity transformed manufacturing. Today, digital technologies are transforming everything.

The scope of this transformation is truly astonishing. It's not surprising that many companies find the challenges of digital business transformation overwhelming. That's why this book is so important. It's a practical guide for navigating the rough waters ahead of us.

This book is also a potent reminder that genuine transformation is always about people and about providing tangible opportunities for real growth. Transformation is a process, and it moves along a fairly predictable path. This book will help you stick to the path and not get distracted.

From my perspective, transformation enables and empowers companies to utilize both customer data and performance data to create new revenue lines that are both vertically and horizontally integrated. Transformation sets the stage for creating new business models and new forms of commerce.

Digital transformation is necessary for success and survival in today's economy, since every company can be considered a technology company and a potential competitor. The explosion of digital technology has opened the floodgates for new entrants in every sector of the global economy, putting every established incumbent and legacy organization at risk.

The prime example of this phenomenon is Amazon, whose brilliant use of data analytics completely disrupted the retail industry. There's a harsh lesson to be learned from Amazon's rise: if existing companies neglect to embrace digital technology, new entrants will certainly attempt to disrupt their business models.

The rapid success of Amazon and other digital disruptors has left many executives in a state of shock. Many organizations seem overwhelmed by the sheer scale of change they face. From the perspective of a traditional company, the challenges can appear insurmountable.

When people feel helpless, they often make rash decisions that prove untenable over time. In their rush to "do something," they make mistakes. Aiming for short-term victories, they sacrifice strategic goals. Reading this book will help you overcome whatever natural sense of panic you might be feeling. This book will help you slow down and thoughtfully consider the logical steps of business transformation.

From my perspective, the best approach is setting reasonable milestones and focusing on incremental gains. Establish measurable and specific key performance indicators (KPIs), benchmarks or milestones that will guide you gradually toward success.

Don't just say, "We want transformation." Instead, decide what transformation looks like to you and how you will get there. Develop a plan ahead of time and stick to it—but don't be afraid to update it as you move along your transformation journey. Cultivate trusted partners to help you execute. Revisit your transformation strategy regularly to keep growing far into the future.

The power of technology is both exciting and compelling. Helping other people recognize what an effective strategy can create for them and seeing them getting excited about it—that's a great feeling.

We all love to read and hear about success stories, where everything works. This book will help you and your stakeholders write your own success stories.

Some people ask me, "What's next? What comes after transformation?" Frankly, I believe the next big challenge will be answering the same questions that successful, forward-thinking companies have always been asking:

> How can we provide further opportunities for our employees, our experts, our leaders, and our creative thinkers to grow and develop?

How can we strengthen the relationship between the corporation and the people it serves, its employees, and the larger community?

These basic questions haven't changed—the best companies are always looking toward the future. What will change, however, are the ways we work toward achieving our goals, using the knowledge and resources available to us through digital business transformation.

This book is an important step toward achieving a better future, and I am confident that you will enjoy reading it.

Arup Das
CEO, Alphaserve Technologies

PREFACE

We've all heard and read that digital transformation is changing our lives. But how precisely are we being transformed? Which aspects of our lives are changing and why does digital transformation matter? Why should you read this book? More specifically, why should you read this book right now?

Digital transformation and digital disruption are urgent concerns for all of us, all over the world. Together they have become an inexorable force of nature. Even if your organization is operating smoothly and hitting its numbers today, I can guarantee you will experience transformation and disruption in the near future.

Elon Musk talks about sending people to Mars. On every imaginable level, the act of colonizing another planet would profoundly transform human culture. Yet we are already deep into the process of transforming humanity.

For the past 100 years, we have been shifting steadily from a culture based primarily on physical labor to a culture based primarily on intellectual labor. In recent decades, the shift has been accelerated by the availability of high-speed computing and broadband communications networks, and by the emergence of data science techniques that have led to the development of practical artificial intelligence.

Soon, the knowledge workers who replaced physical laborers will be at risk of being replaced by AI bots. With alarming speed, we are transitioning from a carbon-based to a silicon-based civilization. This transformation is not a trivial matter.

Definition of Work Is Changing

Within an extremely brief span of time, everything we think of as "work" will be performed by physical or digital robots (scripts) guided by artificial intelligence. Any kind of repetitive task that can be automated will be automated. For human beings, work will become a blend of complex abstract reasoning and pure creativity. In other words, people will only do work that machines are incapable of performing.

What kind of work will we do? Anything that requires creativity, imagination, tenderness, affection, empathy, or love. We will be creators, innovators, inventors, entrepreneurs, artists, poets, teachers, athletes, gamers, healers, caregivers and lifelong learners.

This is not science fiction or fanciful thinking. We're no longer on the cusp of a new era. We are experiencing the opening act of a fundamental shift. Some parts of the world will arrive at this future state sooner than others. But this is our shared destiny, and we need to prepare for it.

That's the big picture, in broad strokes. The rest of this book is about the details of getting from our present state to our digital future. This book is neither a roadmap nor a theoretical treatise. It falls somewhere in between.

I'm perturbed by pundits who make false comparisons between the digital transformation we're facing today and transformations of the past. The digital disruption I'm writing about will shake the foundations of society. It will truly rock our world and change our lives. Most of those changes will be for the better. But many of the changes will leave us feeling lost and confused.

Digital transformation will create millions of new jobs. From a global perspective, I am optimistic and enthusiastic about our future. Yet I am also a realist, and I know that transformation will eliminate jobs and disrupt the careers of people in many sectors of the global economy.

"A digital tsunami is coming," says Chetan Dube, a thought leader in artificial intelligence and the chief executive officer of IPsoft. "Overall, it's a benign tsunami. But it's like a 100-foot wall of water coming toward us. It will sweep away many of the ordinary chores and tasks we do at work. It will remove drudgery from our lives, freeing us to become our best and most creative selves. But we cannot simply sit on the beach and wait for the tsunami to hit us. We must prepare. We must move to higher ground."

Do Not Ignore the Emotional Component

Moving to higher ground requires leaving behind anything that isn't required for immediate survival. As leaders of transformation, it's our responsibility to help people overcome the emotional obstacles they will invariably face as they shed their old work habits and adopt new methods for achieving their goals in the modern workplace.

The process of moving from the familiar past into an unknown future is difficult, to say the least. Ignoring the emotional component would be a sign of poor leadership, and a clear invitation to failure.

I had a wonderful conversation with my friend and colleague, Ben Richards. Ben is the worldwide chief strategy officer at Ogilvy, and he has vast experience helping major brands that are grappling with business transformation strategies.

Here's a brief summary of what Ben told me:

There are two ways of doing transformation; one that sets you up for catastrophe and another that usually works out quite well. The first way is to sit everyone down and offer them an extraordinarily rational explanation of your transformation strategy. That approach almost always paves the road to ruin.

The second approach is explaining to people how the strategy will impact them as individuals. Tell them how it will affect their income and their career. Explain how the strategy will help them become more successful, more fulfilled, and more satisfied.

Given the choice, Ben says, he would "pick the emotional argument over the rational argument any day of the week."

He also recommends reaching out to all the stakeholders in the organization, especially those in the trenches and on the front lines. Make sure that you understand and address their fears and concerns. "You need to win the hearts and minds of your constituents," Ben says.

The last thing you need during a transformation, he says, is a dissatisfied workforce. "If you think that analysts won't call your employees and ask them off the record how the transformation is going, you are mistaken," he says.

Ben advocates in favor of an approach he calls "Platform, Program, Pulse." In this approach, a transformational strategy is divided into time horizons:

Platform = Long Term

Program = Medium Term

Pulse = Short Term

It's not too different from the idea of going for quick victories while you keep your eye on the long-range goal. I also like how the Platform/Program/Pulse model gives you breathing room. Instead of attempting to do everything all at once, you establish a logical timeline for accomplishing the various parts of your transformation strategy.

I genuinely admire Ben's approach, and I urge you to keep it in mind as you move through the stages of your own transformational efforts.

Ecosystems of Disruption

It's also imperative to remember that transformation and disruption do not occur in a vacuum. At the risk of stating the obvious, everything is connected. Instead of thinking about transformation and disruption as free-standing events, I urge you to envision them as constituent parts of a much larger and continually evolving ecosystem of organizations and their stakeholders.

I found the experience of Goran Kukic, head of IT innovation at Nestlé, to be highly instructive. In a wide-ranging conversation, Kukic described how Nestlé built a specific program for dealing with the startup community, which is a prime source of disruptive innovation and transformation.

"Dealing with a startup can be exceptionally challenging," Kukic says. "You can't send a 40-page contract to a startup. They are simply not traditional companies."

Even when there are clear business reasons for collaborating, cultural mismatches between startups and traditional companies can lead to disastrous relationships. To improve the odds of success, Nestlé created a Silicon Valley Innovation Outpost to scout opportunities for collaboration and build essential relationships on the ground.

"We realized there was so much more to be learned from startups," he says. Today, Nestlé has a team of innovation managers in the San Francisco Bay area. They have become familiar faces in the startup community; they are part of the landscape.

From my perspective, Nestlé's approach is absolutely brilliant. Instead of regarding innovation, disruption, and transformation as alien or unnatural, the company sees them as natural and integral to continuing success.

Hope for the Best, Prepare for the Worst

Part of our general uneasiness about digital disruption, however, arises from our sense that it is occurring quite suddenly. In fact, it is the tail of a larger transformation that's been going on since the beginning of the twentieth century. We tend to think of the most recent advances in technology as being the most significant and the most influential, but the reality is more nuanced. Each of the previous advances was essential, and we wouldn't be where we are today without them.

Moreover, the pace of transformation has been logarithmic, not linear. Each of the five advances in computing can be rightfully considered a paradigm shift, and each advance contributed exponentially to the growth of computing power.

I mention this because it's important to dispel any notions that digital transformation is some kind of magical event or sudden break with the past. Digital transformation is both a powerful force and a natural leap forward in a process that's been going on for quite a while.

If digital transformation is merely another step in a natural process, why do so many people find it confusing? The answer is simple and somewhat embarrassing: the business technology community has done a less than stellar job of explaining what digital transformation is and how it will affect the lives of everyday people.

A world-renowned creative leader who works with technology companies on defining their brands puts it eloquently:

We talk about digital transformation and we know it's coming, but nobody really knows what it means, it's a loose term. Most of us don't know exactly how digital transformation will change our lives and our jobs, so we assume the worst.

His comments echo the sentiments of many people we interviewed for this book. I cannot offer answers to the existential questions raised about digital transformation. I will, however, provide specific steps and processes for assuring the best possible outcomes from your business transformation efforts.

We do not live in a deterministic universe. I do not believe the future is carved in stone. Technology is a tool and we get to choose how we want to use it. This book lays out some of the choices. It offers suggestions for moving forward in a thoughtful and responsible manner. I hope you find this book helpful in your transformation journey.

I conclude my introduction with wise words from Lauren Crampsie, president, Ogilvy New York:

Change of any kind, digital or human, is always about managing expectations, setting goals and defining clear responsibilities for executing against those objectives. Given the pace of change today, organizations have to respond with a tenacity which often means questioning every precedent and definitely changing the status quo.

ACKNOWLEDGMENTS

Thank you to all my colleagues, friends, and advisors for sharing of your precious time and brilliance to this project; this body of work would not be the same without your real-life experiences and inputs: Mitra Best, Lauren Crampsie, Chetan Dube, Sonia Fernandes, Anna Frazetto, Steve Goldstein, Nalini Guhesh, Carla Hendra, Nikhil Jinghan, Goran Kukic, Adam Morris, Ben Richards, Rajesh Sinha, Atle Skjekkeland, R. Sridhar, Steve Sterin, Jonathan Stern, Tiger Tyagarajan, Phil Wiser, and Sigal Zarmi.

Special thanks to Arup Das, Vineet Jain, Thornton May, and Meredith Whalen for your extended contribution, counsel, and the immeasurable amounts of time that you offered to this endeavor.

Special thanks to Mike Barlow for your patience in the writing process and helping me keep it real.

And thanks to Sheck Cho, who made this project possible.

Chapter 1

Drivers of Change

Executive Summary: The world is changing rapidly and organizations need to adapt to survive. Transformation is an essential and inevitable process of business evolution, requiring hard decisions about the allocation of limited resources. Assembling the right team of people is primary to success; the technology is secondary.

Thanks to Clayton Christensen, we're all familiar with the concept of disruption. In his classic bestseller, *The Innovator's Dilemma*, Christensen describes the fate of major companies that don't foresee the impact of disruption on their business models.

The disrupted companies were not run by fools. For the most part, their executives were intelligent, skilled, and experienced business leaders. With the luxury of 20-20 hindsight, it's easy for us to shake our heads and wonder why they missed the signals that foretold their demise.

We cannot change the past. But we can influence the future. My advice to everyone reading this book is to dust off your copy of *The Innovator's Dilemma* and read it again. This time, ask yourself if your organization is a likely target for disruption.

Here's a quick pass-fail test to determine if your organization is a candidate for disruption:

- Have you digitized all of your business processes?
- Are you collecting data from all your business processes?
- Are you analyzing the data you collect?
- Are you optimizing your processes based on insights generated by your analysis of the data?

If you answered "no" to any of the questions above, you must consider your organization a candidate for disruption.

Here's the plain unvarnished truth: if your organization is not on a path to having working digital version of every critical process it performs, your organization will be disrupted and in all likelihood will fail.

Today, every business-to-consumer (B2C) organization understands that simple fact. It's digital or die. That's why

B2C companies are racing to provide their customers with the best possible digital experiences.

The smarter business-to-business (B2B) firms also understand this, but you would be surprised how many are lagging. The bad news for them: the digital laggards will fail or at the very least fall behind those who have indeed threaded that needle. They will be unable to compete in a world in which the majority of their potential customers want to interact with your website before they talk with anyone from your sales team.

"Millennials don't want to have a conversation with your sales team, they want to have a conversation with your website," says Adam Morris, CEO of Redstage, a strategy and design consulting firm specializing in B2B ecommerce.

It's easy to pick on millennials, and the demographic is mischaracterized in almost every conversation. I've heard countless complaints about how this demographic doesn't want to communicate. That's unfounded rhetoric. Millennials definitely want to communicate using their medium of their choice. They're constantly communicating via text and social media. They are avid users of collaboration platforms like Slack, RingCentral Glip, Snapchat, Instagram, Fuze, ChatBlazer, Workplace by Facebook, and Skype.

If your organization still relies primarily on phone and email, you've missed the boat. Even if the majority of your customers aren't millennials, it's fair to say the majority of your customers are influenced by them. According to a Pew Research Center analysis of U.S. Census Bureau data, millennials are already the largest generation in the workforce. Can you really afford to write off their influence?

I have business acquaintances who tell me their best customers are "an older demographic" who don't text, won't use a collaboration platform, and don't care about their user interface. They tell me they won't invest in mobile apps and better UIs because "young people" aren't interested in buying their products and services, so why bother?

Complaints of that nature are self-destructive and self-fulfilling. Any organization that ignores the habits and preferences of an entire generation of potential customers is writing its own epitaph.

In later chapters of this book, I write about the imperative for enabling collaboration and communication across the modern enterprise. A global business in the twenty-first century bears little resemblance to businesses of the past. Back in the day, everything was about command and control. Power and influence were highly concentrated. Information was shared on a strictly "need-to-know" basis.

Today's business climate favors decentralized and distributed operations. Nowadays, we understand that information is an asset that grows in value when shared. There is nothing more useless than so-called "dark data," which is a term for data that is collected and never put to work.

Moreover, there is a high probability that a significant portion of your workforce works remotely or outside of traditional business hours. If you're not making it easy for them to communicate and exchange information, their value to the organization is greatly reduced.

Brass Ring or Black Hole?

After you've finished reading *The Innovator's Dilemma*, take up Geoffrey Moore's book *Zone to Win: Organizing to Compete in an Age of Disruption*. I'm sure that most of you have read Moore's first book, *Crossing the Chasm*. By now, the book's basic message is well known. It feels familiar and comfortable.

Zone to Win will reawaken your sense of urgency. It will make you feel uncomfortable again, which is precisely how you should feel if you want your digital transformation strategy to succeed.

Remember, the majority of transformation projects fail to meet expectations. A landmark McKinsey survey revealed that only 26% of respondents said their transformational efforts were "very or completely" successful. That failure rate represents "a $900 billion hole in enterprise strategy" according to a recent Forbes post.

My back-of-the-envelope explanation for why most transformations fail is simple: the failed projects focused on fuzzy long-term objectives when they should have focused on precise short- and medium-term objectives. Their vision exceeded their grasp and strategy certainly exceeds their ability to execute.

The irony is that short-term victories can lead to long-term advantages, especially in turbulent markets and uncertain economic conditions. There's a good reason for not losing a view of the larger strategic picture while also focusing on the now; with any luck, it will sustain you long enough to beat back your fiercest competitors.

Digital transformation can be the brass ring that keeps you riding merrily on the carousel. Or it can be a black hole that drains your resources and ends your career.

In my case, I've had the good fortune of transformation initiatives helping my career. That's because I approached every transformation with a sharp sense of trepidation and a deep reservoir of humility. I'm not embarrassed to admit when I am skittish about a plan. In many instances, fear can be a strong motivator. Fear reminds us to proceed with care and caution.

I've found it beneficial to be a hands-on' executive. I work closely with our internal teams. I work directly with our vendor partners and solution providers. I am familiar with the technologies that we develop and deploy in our transformational projects. And the buck always stops with me.

The amazing success and longevity of Chuck Yeager, one of the world's greatest test pilots, is attributed partly to his superlative flying skills and partly to his hands-on mechanical understanding of the aircraft he flew. Yeager took the time to become familiar with the parts and pieces of the airplanes that carried him aloft.

When something went wrong or didn't feel quite right, Yeager knew how to handle it. His deep technical knowledge and keen understanding of aviation systems were absolutely fundamental to his achievements, and he is a role model personally for me and for all of us who labor in the trenches of digital transformation.

Mechanics of Transformation

One of the lessons we learn from Chuck Yeager's career is the importance of understanding the fundamental mechanics of a solution. Gaining this level of understanding requires getting in the weeds and getting your hands dirty. You cannot manage a transformation from afar. You need to be right there, in close touch with the teams who are making it happen.

Additionally, you must be prepared to answer questions—dozens and perhaps hundreds of questions from internal and external stakeholders at every level who are affected by your transformation projects. Inevitably, people will ask, "Why are we doing this? Why are we transforming these processes and disrupting our traditional ways of operating? Why are we changing?"

When these types of question arise, this book will help you provide reasonable answers. It's written for the purpose of helping you navigate through the multiple nuances of transformation and cope effectively with the shocks and surprises that will occur as you move forward toward your goal.

Here's something I learned from my experiences as an agent of transformation: although change is natural, it doesn't feel natural. Some people are exhilarated by change, but most people find it upsetting. As a leader, you need to accept this fact. You have been chosen to lead a transformation initiative because you are the outlier – the person who actually enjoys change! No matter what anyone tells you, they do not share your degree of enthusiasm. They are not optimistic. They are fearful.

One of your primary responsibilities is managing their fears and allaying their suspicions that your transformational effort will make their lives more difficult or result in the elimination of their jobs.

These are not idle worries. They will prey on the minds of the people you lead, and you must address these concerns forthrightly and without equivocation. As Franklin Delano Roosevelt famously said, "The only thing we have to fear is fear itself."

One of the most successful techniques used by NASA to prepare astronauts for the challenges of space missions is familiarization through continual training and simulation.

NASA prepares its astronauts so thoroughly for their missions that by the time they go into space, they've already practiced the mission hundreds of time on Earth. NASA takes exquisite care to make sure that its astronauts are ready for anything that could possibly happen.

I urge you to adopt similar practices. Prepare your people for transformation. Walk them slowly and carefully through the steps. Encourage them to ask questions. Reward them for offering ideas and suggestions for making the transformation process go more smoothly and efficiently.

Whenever possible, turn your transformation projects into team activities so they feel more like games than work. I'm sure I don't have to explain to you the importance of gamification. If there's an aspect of a transformation project that can by gamified, by all means, gamify it!

Levels of Transformation

Reading *Zone to Win* reminded me that transformation can occur at three different levels. At the first level, transformation focuses on upgrading and streamlining foundational technologies and infrastructure. At the second level, transformation improves the efficiency and throughput of standard business operations and processes. At the third level, however, transformation helps the organization create and enable new business models.

Some people might argue that newly minted organizations with no legacy infrastructure can safely ignore the first two levels of transformation, but I would counter by arguing that infrastructure and operations will always require close attention, even when they're delivered as services in the cloud.

Organizations encounter obstacles and frustrations at each level of transformation. Ask any organization with poor foundational infrastructure how their transformation is going and you will receive feedback in no uncertain terms. However, the critical challenges fall into two broad categories: people and processes.

Let's tackle the "people challenge" first, since it invariably poses the greatest danger to any transformation initiative. "People are afraid of change," says Atle Skjekkeland, president of the Digital Value Institute. Appealing to their emotions probably won't work, since their fears are likely to overwhelm the "rational" explanations you offer to prove that change is necessary.

Fortunately, "you don't need the majority of people to be on your side, only a handful of key individuals who see the value in your transformation project," Skjekkeland says.

The idea of "key individuals" surfaced repeatedly in the interviews I conducted when researching and writing this book. My own experience has taught me that transformation is not a popularity contest. You don't require a majority to succeed—you need the support of top executives, key influencers, and a hand-picked team of "transformers" to carry out the project. "We put our best people on the project, and they're committed for the duration," says Steven Sterin, a Fortune 100 CFO and senior executive with decades of experience. "You want the best people, working full-time on the project."

Processes are the next challenge. Installing new technology is pointless unless it's accompanied by new processes enabling people to use it easily and effectively. Remember, the success or failure of any transformation project is judged by its adoption rate. People need methods that will allow them to get the most out of the new tech investment.

Human beings have instinctive abilities to judge value, and they'll know immediately if a transformational project has made their lives better or worse. If a new method makes their lives easier, they'll use it readily. If it makes their lives harder, they'll find ways to avoid using it. The long tail of any transformation is adoption by your target audience.

It's also important to remember that transformational projects have costs. That might seem obvious, but it's a simple truth that is often forgotten in the heat of battle. In *Zone to Win*, Moore writes primarily about disruption, yet his basic message also applies to transformation. He notes that "to disrupt someone else's business, you have to add a net new line of business to your own portfolio."

Since neither your portfolio nor your budget is infinitely expandable, you are forced to make hard choices. Do you shift resources from an existing line of business to fund a new line of business? How do you explain and rationalize that shift of resources? Are you willing to sacrifice short-term returns in favor of long-term goals?

Transformational leaders face the same questions and are forced to make similarly difficult choices. Let's say you're planning to move an application into the cloud and significantly reduce your budget. Moving infrastructure into the cloud isn't free; whichever cloud provider you choose—whether it's AWS, Microsoft Azure, Google, IBM, or another company—will charge you a substantial fee for the privilege of using their platforms.

But that's only the financial side of the picture. At some point soon after making your decision, you'll need to have the difficult conversation with your technology staff about structural changes to support the new model.

We talk and write frequently about people, process, and technology being the essential components of transformation. I would add a fourth component: executive leadership. You need more than just technical acumen to lead a transformation. You need courage, empathy, foresight, patience, self-discipline, and enthusiasm. Yes, those are "soft skills." Over the long game, however, they are the critical skills you need to succeed as a transformational leader.

"Having driven—and reacted to—many disruptive market shifts in media in both startups and major media corporations,

I have found that true digital transformation only comes from persistent and consistent leadership toward a new model of people, product and business drivers. This type of transformation is not a single big bang project," says Phil Wiser, chief technology officer of the CBS Corporation.

On the Ground and in the Trenches

I couldn't agree more with Mr. Wiser; my experience leads me to believe that digital transformation is only the starting point for an extended series of processes. Transformation is a long game—that is indisputable.

Transformation usually begins in the back office, yet its true impact is felt across the organization. A genuinely successful transformation strategy will have ripple effects spreading far beyond the traditional boundaries of your company. Even small or highly specialized projects can have global effects.

At a recent gathering of design thinkers for a company that makes jet engines, I was pleasantly surprised to find that portions of the engine design were developed through crowdsourcing platforms. Design thinking has the potential to create entirely new dimensions of innovation. From my perspective, it's a form of transformation.

I foresee enormous transformational power in the emerging DARQ stack. *DARQ* is the acronym for distributed ledger technology (DLT), artificial intelligence (AI), extended reality (XR), and quantum computing (QC). Even if the acronym fades from usage, the underlying technologies will be with us for a quite a while, transforming a wide variety of services in multiple industries. DARQ will lead to a new generation of services in areas such as predictive maintenance, real-time payments, just-in-time manufacturing, multi-modal transportation, education, public safety, healthcare and biotechnology.

The Internet of Things (IoT) has similar transformational potential, especially in terms of enabling the rapid development of smart homes, smart schools, smart power grids, smart roads, smart towns, smart cities, smart regions, and even smart nations.

I conclude this chapter with a counterintuitive notion suggested by my friend Tiger Tyagarajan, the visionary CEO of Genpact. Tiger is an industry leader who pioneered a new global business model and transformed a division of GE (formerly GE Capital International Services) into Genpact, a remarkably successful global professional services firm focused on delivering digital transformation for its clients. Here is his observation:

> *When something is running well, that's often the best time to change it. It seems so counterintuitive, but the notion of always finding a better way to do something is at the core of our cultural ethos.*

Net Takeaways

1. Transformation is not optional; it's an imperative driven by factors and conditions beyond your control. Ultimately, transformation brings you to a better place, but the journey is difficult.

2. Transformation is not a popularity contest. You don't require a majority to succeed—you need the support of top executives, key influencers, and a hand-picked team of your best people to carry out the project.

3. Leading a successful transformation requires more than technical know-how; it requires a blend of "soft skills," including empathy, patience, and self-discipline.

4. Transformation isn't limited by traditional corporate boundaries; there are ripple effects that spread widely across multiple industries and economic sectors.

Chapter 2

Focus and Discipline

Executive Summary: In this chapter, we examine the importance of a focused mindset, thorough training, clarity of purpose, and quick responses. We also introduce a helpful technique for demystifying leadership decisions and sharing priorities.

All of us, no matter who we are or where we come from, face adversity in our lives. Adversity can be a great teacher.

I was raised in a small fishing village on the outskirts of Mumbai, one of India's largest and most populated cities. Our home was tiny, about 100 square feet. There were seven of us: my parents and grandmother, me, and three siblings. We had no running water. Every morning at 4:30 a.m., before he went to work, my father would bring four empty buckets to the community tap, fill them with water, and bring them back home. Three buckets were for washing, cleaning, cooking, and other daily chores. The fourth bucket was for drinking. Since we had no refrigerator, we poured our drinking water into an earthen pot. That's how we kept it cool during the day.

I'm sharing this story because it taught me several valuable lessons. I learned from an early age that resources are precious and must be managed carefully. I learned that when you have limited choices, you can devise workarounds and alternatives that will serve your purposes.

I also learned that I did not wish to spend the rest of my life in poverty. My father worked for a company that printed labels on tubes of toothpaste. As a child, I found the process of printing colorful labels on shiny metal tubes absolutely fascinating. By village standards, my father had a good job at a solid company. But I had a strong desire to explore opportunities beyond the village, to attend a different school or travel to another country—a goal that seemed so elusive at that young age and in those surroundings.

I often say my first financial advisor was my grandmother. When I was seven, she took me to our local bank and opened an account in my name. She deposited 20 rupees, the equivalent of about 10 cents, into the account. Opening an account made me feel very special and I vividly remember the exhilarating feeling of walking into the "big" bank building with many ceiling fans and glass counters. I didn't realize that I was at the beginning of a long journey that would eventually take me far from home.

In addition to being a wise financial counselor, my grand-mother was a great typist. She worked for our local church, typing up notes, sermons, and announcements. She had a Remington typewriter, a manual machine with mechanical keys and ribbon spools. She was fast and accurate—80 words per minute, never a mistake. I remember her clacking away at the keys, slamming the carriage return lever and feeding fresh sheets of paper into the roller. I marveled at her skill and dexterity.

But what I remember most was her discipline. She sat down at her typewriter and stayed there until she completed her task. That's what really impressed me. She always finished what she started. Her focus was unshakeable.

I didn't know it at the time, but my grandmother was teaching me important lessons. Discipline and focus are essential for success. Always finish what you start, whether you're typing up a newsletter or deploying an enterprise technology platform. Nothing will kill your chances for success faster than quitting before the job is done. The subtle lesson from my grandmother was: don't quit. Keep striving until you reach your goals.

Brace for Impact

Discipline and focus are key ingredients of success. But you also need training, knowledge, and experience to make the most of your opportunities when they arise. In my case, this was especially true.

In early 2009, I was promoted to my first global leadership role as a CIO. It was during the depths of the Great Recession. The stock market had already fallen precipitously and was still heading down. The world was struggling and there was no light at the end of the tunnel.

I felt particularly beleaguered. There I was, in a new job at a multinational company where I was expected to oversee large investments and implement major changes. Instead, the collapse of the global economy had pulled the rug out from under me. Like many other people at that time, I was uncertain about the future. Despite the turmoil around us, my superiors had high hopes and great expectations. But how could I deliver on their expectations in a shrinking economy? From my perspective, the future looked grim.

Then a miraculous event occurred. On January 15, 2009, US Airways Flight 1549 struck a flock of geese and lost power in both engines shortly after takeoff from LaGuardia Airport in New York City. Minutes after losing power, the plane touched down safely in the Hudson River. There were a few injuries, but everyone on the plane survived. The emergency water landing was hailed as the most successful ditching of an airplane in aviation history.

So much has been written about the "Miracle on the Hudson" that I don't feel it's necessary to recount the details. Suffice it to say the swift and effective responses of pilots Chesley "Sully" Sullenberger and Jeffrey Skiles turned a potential tragedy into a galvanizing moment.

Unexpectedly, the world experienced a sudden jolt of optimism. It was like someone had turned on a light. In a flash, we saw that even our most our difficult problems were manageable. We felt inspired and reinvigorated.

As an aviation enthusiast, I wanted to know how Sully had saved the day. After watching the news reports on television and reading dozens of articles, I came to believe the miracle could be encapsulated in three words spoken by Sully to his crew: "Brace for impact."

For the crew of Flight 1549, those three simple words lit the fuse. All their years of practice and training kicked into high gear. They knew exactly what they needed to do, and they did it. Moreover, Sully knew the crewmembers would perform their duties, leaving him free to fly the aircraft to a safe landing in the river.

There are many lessons we can learn from Flight 1549. For me, the main takeaway is that you need a combination of personal skills and a well-trained team supporting you. When you've properly trained your team, they know their duties and responsibilities. You don't have to micromanage them. You have the freedom to focus on what lies ahead. That's what true leadership is all about. Leaders guide their teams and their organizations into the future.

Like many people, I was moved and inspired by the safe landing of Flight 1549. I felt new confidence, and I resolved to move ahead decisively with my plans for transforming and improving our global operations. The rest, as they say, is history.

Our mission was successful. Over the following years, we brought many new technologies into our portfolio and deployed numerous systems. We executed our duties with tremendous focus, raised the bar with every small success, fulfilled our responsibilities, and created opportunities for greater success down the road.

During this period of time, I developed my own version of the matrix used by President Dwight Eisenhower and later adapted by Dr Stephen Covey to prioritize decisions. The matrix is invaluable to IT leaders for two critical reasons:

1. It becomes a visual tool for prioritizing projects.

2. It clarifies your intentions to the team.

The first reason is largely self-explanatory. It's almost always easier to grasp complex plans when they are displayed visually. That's a simple fact of human nature.

The second reason is more complex. When you are leading a digital transformation, your intentions must be absolutely crystal clear to everyone on the team. The people you're depending on to get the job done must know what's happening and why. They need to know what's on your mind. They need to know where they fit in the larger picture.

The matrix is a useful tool for conveying your priorities at a glance. I've found that it's the key to achieving alignment of

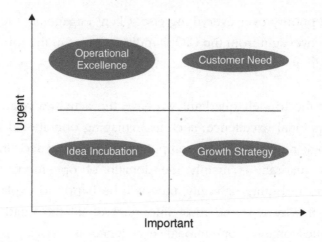

Figure 2.1 Urgent vs. Important matrix.

purpose. All it takes is one quick look at the matrix to know immediately where you stand.

My version of the matrix is shown in Figure 2.1. Please take a moment to consider how it would apply in your situation.

Now let's drill down into the matrix and look at each of the quadrants. I use some variant of the matrix in all of my presentations, and I find it resonates with audiences in every part of the world.

In the example in the figure, the matrix is drawn from the CIO's perspective. Different executive functions would have different labels on the quadrants, but the basic structure of the matrix would be the same across the C-suite.

In the top-right quadrant we have customer and client needs. In all but a few exceptional circumstances, those needs take priority over everything else. Client engagement teams, with oversight from the CIO, handle activities in the top-right quadrant.

In the top-left quadrant we have the activities related to operational excellence, such as managing operational technology, networks, cloud computing, finance and accounting. This quadrant is mainly the domain of operations managers, and quite naturally, they will be happy to explain at length why it is the most important of all the quadrants. Unquestionably, operational excellence is critical, but it rarely takes priority over meeting customer needs.

In the bottom-right quadrant we have activities related to strategy development. This is mostly the domain of business strategists, but the CIO and other senior leaders will be closely involved. This is where new opportunities are identified and new techniques for business growth are developed.

Finally, in the bottom-left quadrant we have incubation, which in many ways is the most necessary of all the business functions. But for practical purposes it takes a backseat to the other quadrants. It would be easy to overlook or downplay the incubation function, but a good leader will make sure it gets the attention it needs. Incubation is where the next great ideas come from. It's the domain of visionary thinking, continuous improvement, invention, and innovation that will take the enterprise to the next level. That's why you cannot ignore the role of incubation.

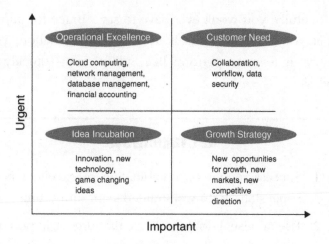

Figure 2.2 Urgent vs. Important matrix with examples.

Figure 2.2 is a version of the matrix with the activities of each quadrant filled in. Remember, this is a hypothetical/ generic matrix. Every organization's matrix will look slightly different. But the purpose of the matrix remains unchanged, no matter where it's applied. Think of it as your North Star, a fixed point in the sky guiding your journey.

The matrix is a useful tool for setting priorities and allocating resources. But I also see it as a technique for demystifying and clarifying the department's duties and responsibilities. It engenders a sense of discipline and makes it easier for your team to focus on what's truly important. The matrix should be incorporated into training processes so the team can respond effectively and without hesitation when problems or emergencies occur.

Hopefully, you won't ever have to say, "Brace for impact." But if you do find yourself in a perilous situation, you'll want your team to perform like Sully's crew—quickly and flawlessly.

Net Takeaways

1. Success requires a combination of excellent personal skills and a well-trained team supporting you.

2. Use a visual tool such as the urgent/important matrix to clarify and demystify your goals and intentions.

3. When your team is properly trained and motivated, you don't have to micromanage them. You have the freedom to focus on the path forward. That's what true leadership is all about—looking ahead and seeking the next challenge.

Chapter 3

Idea Incubation

Executive Summary: In this chapter, we look at the granular details of an incubation process and outline the steps of a practical framework for innovation in the modern enterprise.

It is natural for high-performing organizations to focus on operational excellence. If you can't manage the basics, no one will take you seriously.

At the same time, maintaining the status quo is never enough. We don't wake up in the morning and say, "Today, I want to do exactly what I did yesterday." As social human beings, we know variety is the spice of life. We don't want the same old thing; we long for the excitement of new frontiers and fresh challenges.

In today's hypercompetitive and continually evolving markets, innovation is essential for success. Innovation is more than a frill or a luxury; it's absolutely imperative. Consumers and users expect to see new products and services unveiled at frequent intervals. When they don't see innovation, they suspect something is wrong.

But here's the hard truth: when you're running at full-speed and firing on all cylinders, you don't have time to be innovative. Your first and primary concern is getting the job done as quickly and as effectively as possible. That's the way modern industry works—your pay is based on your performance and your performance is typically judged by operational parameters.

Superstars such as Beyoncé, the singer-songwriter-performer, and Jony Ive, the former chief design officer of Apple, are compensated largely on the basis of their innate creativity. Most of us, however, are paid according to how well we perform our jobs. While the focus on performance is totally understandable from a purely operational perspective, it creates serious challenges for companies that want to be innovative.

Overcoming the Natural Inclination to Avoid Risk

It is also natural for organizations to strive relentlessly for greater efficiency and higher productivity, even when it means sacrificing creativity and originality. In many organizations, the fear of failure outweighs the desire for success. Corporations are intrinsically risk averse; it goes with the territory.

Innovation, however, requires taking risks. Being innovative means exploring new ground, going where no one has gone before, pushing the envelope, and leaping into the unknown.

"Innovation is like parenting," says Nikhil Jhingan, a serial innovator who has developed many new products and solutions. "A new idea is like a child," he says. "To the outside world, the child might not seem particularly useful. But the parents of the child see its potential. They nurture and protect the child. With their help, the child blossoms into a magnificent human being, accomplishes wonderful things, and changes the world."

Like children, no two ideas are exactly alike; each must be treated differently. As a result, there is no ironclad procedure for innovating and no single path to perfection. Each idea requires a unique approach.

For example, devising a solution to address a commonly recognized problem can be handled by a committee because there's a strong likelihood that everyone is seeking the same result. Even if you don't know exactly what the solution will look like, there is already agreement over its purpose.

However, developing a truly visionary solution to address a highly complex problem will probably require a strong internal champion to clear a path and protect the idea in its nascent stages. "When an idea is really visionary, you need an empowered champion at a high level of the organization to make it happen," Jhingan says.

In any case, innovation rarely proceeds in a straight line. "It's more of a rollercoaster," he says. "There are ups and downs. It can be scary and unnerving. For every success, you experience many failures."

You Can't Just Wing It

Because there is an inherent conflict between the day-to-day operational goals of the organization and the need for innovation, formal processes are necessary to make certain that innovation is encouraged, cultivated, nurtured, and protected.

When I speak to smaller groups at professional conferences, I often conduct a nonscientific poll by asking members of the audience to raise their hands if their organizations have formal innovation processes. At a typical conference, very few people raise their hands. I often follow up by asking if they believe that innovation processes can be formalized or structured. Again, only a few respond affirmatively.

The lack of affirmative responses goes a long way toward explaining why so many companies struggle with innovation. From my point of view, there are no legitimate reasons for not developing and implementing processes for supporting and promoting continuous innovation.

It is myopic to assume that you cannot put frameworks, guardrails, and guidelines around creativity. Processes are necessary, even when you're thinking creatively, because they don't affect the idea itself but provide a method to convert the idea into a product or service.

For example, the incubator process we developed has become fundamental to our ability to innovate continuously. Our incubator methodology is both rigorous and flexible.

Why are rigor and flexibility both important? Rigor is necessary to keep the process on track, moving forward and generating practical solutions at a steady pace. Flexibility is required to accommodate sudden or unexpected shifts (internally or externally) demanding quick responses. Since the overarching goal is driving and enabling innovation, the processes cannot be overly fixed or rigid—they must be adjustable and adaptable.

Inside the Incubator

Let's take a look at how the incubation process works. This isn't something that was developed overnight—it required years of experimentation and many mistakes before we got it right.

We knew from the start that our mission would be developing products and services that would make a substantive difference to the enterprise. In addition to being effective and impactful, the timing had to be right. We weren't looking for pie in the sky; we focused on creating solutions with tangible and timely benefits. The solutions we created also needed to be easily and readily scalable, since our firm operated in

168 locations around the world. Additionally, we knew that if a solution proved successful and was adopted widely, we would need to provide versions in at least seven different languages.

Initially, we held two working sessions per year. Each meeting lasted two days. We invited eight to twelve technology leaders with global or regional responsibilities. Sometimes we invited marketing leaders to join the conversation. We had an agenda and predefined topics to cover, based on our perceptions of what kinds of innovation the company would need in the near-term future.

We also had three simple rules for the meetings:

1. Disconnect from operational world.

2. Come with ideas and be ready to speak up.

3. All ideas, big and small, are welcome.

We purposely created a very fast-paced environment, using a whiteboard to capture ideas as they flowed. Maintaining a high level of intensity was important for two reasons. The first reason was that most of the attendees had just flown in from different time zones and invariably many were experiencing jet lag. So we had to keep them focused and energized!

The second reason was engagement—we discovered that setting a quick tempo with rapid-fire dialogue would keep us involved and engaged in the process. We strove to keep the conversations lively, stimulating, and exciting. We wanted everyone's synapses firing continously!

We also set expectations. We welcomed outlandish ideas—as long as they were relevant to our business goals and offered the potential for creating efficiencies or competitive advantages in our markets. In other words, we weren't looking for moonshots. The ideas had to solve problems that were specific to our business.

Even with those guardrails in place, we still had many raucous debates and constructive arguments. To an outsider, the first morning session would have seemed chaotic. There would be open challenges and counterchallenges before we started to streamline the debate. Eventually, we would agree on two or three ideas worth pursuing. Then in the afternoon session, we would settle down and focus on turning at least one of those ideas into a practical solution.

Any ideas that survived the first-morning session became part of our incubator portfolio. The portfolio served as an "idea bank" we could dip into at any time. Over the years, the idea bank has proven extremely useful, providing us with a virtually inexhaustible supply of "seed ideas" we could bring to fruition when the timing was right.

The second day was dedicated to moving quickly from ideation to creation. This is when we shifted from right-brain thinking to left-brain thinking. We allowed our "inner engineers" to emerge. We worked together as a closely knit team to devise a solution that was viable, sustainable, and scalable.

We pressed ahead briskly, racing against our self-imposed 5 p.m. deadline. Our breaks were short and the caffeine and pizza was plentiful. Our diet wasn't ideal, but our minds were fully engaged on solving the problem at hand.

Over time, the incubator sessions became popular hackathons. Being selected to attend a session was considered a privilege. For a while, we held them on a quarterly basis before expanding to regional centers as well.

Most important, however, is that we succeeded in developing and implementing a process for generating a steady stream of fresh ideas and new solutions that helped the company achieve its business objectives.

The QRate Template

Our incubation process is supportive and nurturing. It encourages ideation in a collaborative environment. We want our teams to know their ideas are both valuable and valued.

That said, I would never describe our incubation process as warm and fuzzy. Projects are not allowed to drag on ad infinitum; there are boundaries and timelines. No proposals are sacrosanct; each idea must sink or swim based on its own merit.

There are limits to how much you can brainstorm before you need to begin testing your assumptions. Setting a cadence, establishing momentum, and generating observable outcomes are critical. Realizing the need for structure, we created a template with discrete steps and distinct phases. We call it the QRate Model, and it outlines a process for rating the queue of ideas in our incubator. Figure 3.1 is a diagram of the full model.

Now let's break it down into its component parts and see how it works in practice.

The model incorporates three basic phases:

1. Create

2. Validate

3. Build

Each phase has two subphases:

1. Create

    o Ideate

    o Test concept

2. Validate

    o Pilot

    o Validate results

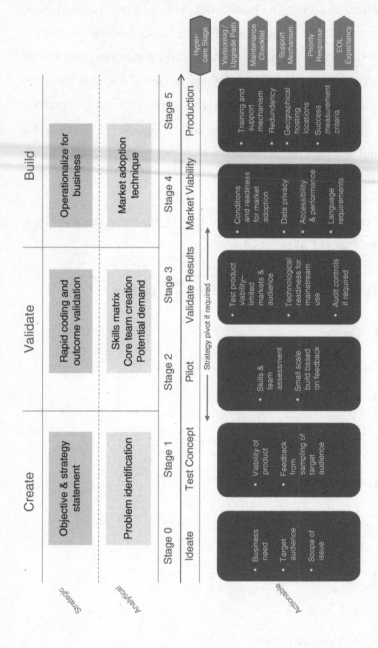

Figure 3.1 The QRate Model.

3. Build

   o Market viability

   o Production

Each subphase has two or more action steps:

- Ideate

   o Business need

   o Target audience

   o Scope of issue

- Test Concept

   o Viability of product

   o Feedback from sampling target audience

- Pilot

   o Skills and team assessment

   o Small-scale build based on assessment

   o Pivot if necessary

- Validate Results

   o Test product viability in limited markets and audiences

   o Technological readiness for mainstream use

   o Audit controls if required

- Market Viability

   o Conditions and readiness for market adoption

   o Data privacy

- o Accessibility and performance

- o Language requirements

- Production

  - o Training and support mechanism

  - o Redundancy

  - o Geographical hosting locations

  - o Success measurement criteria

When you're leading or guiding an incubator process, it's important to remember that you always have at least two audiences.

- Strategic audience: C-level, board, and senior executives
- Analytic audience: Directors, managers, and developers

You will need to communicate differently with each of these two audiences, since each has its own interests and priorities. The strategic audience doesn't necessarily need to hear all the details, but it needs to see the big picture and understand the overall financial impact of your project. Its buy-in is essential for a variety of reasons, including financial support and dealing with potential obstacles that could slow down or derail the project.

The analytic audience, which includes users, needs to know the details, since they are the key to adoption once the solution is rolled out. Without their buy-in, it would be hard to achieve the adoption rates necessary for a successful deployment.

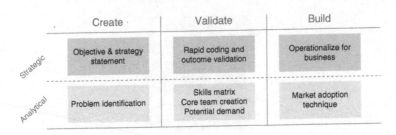

	Create	Validate	Build
Strategic	Objective & strategy statement	Rapid coding and outcome validation	Operationalize for business
Analytical	Problem identification	Skills matrix Core team creation Potential demand	Market adoption technique

Figure 3.2 Actions by audience segmentation.

Figure 3.2 shows a closer view of audience differentiation subprocess.

The template also includes a "Hypercare" stage to manage the solution after it's released (Figure 3.3). Since the ultimate gauge of success is adoption, it's imperative to maintain a close watch on products after they're rolled out and to respond quickly when usage issues arise.

We've used the QRate template to incubate and develop dozens of new solutions over the years. Although every project presents its own unique problems and challenges, the template has proven flexible enough to handle a wide range of ideas. Having a standard process really makes a difference, and it contributes meaningfully to our ability as a company to innovate rapidly and continuously.

The process also serves as a baseline, enabling us to contrast and compare projects over time. Following the template has become a discipline, and it's taught us many valuable lessons.

Figure 3.3 Managing adoption rates through better issue resolution.

Here are five critical lessons we learned from our incubation process:

1. Strive for simplicity. The most successful solutions are usually the simplest and most straightforward.

2. Test, test, test. And make sure to conduct your tests with real people, not just with scripts or bots.

3. Seek feedback from as many sources as possible. Objective, unemotional feedback is unadulterated rocket fuel for your initiative.

4. Include project management experts in the process from its earliest stages. Do not fear the project management office (PMO); work closely with the PMO and leverage

its strengths and knowledge as you progress through the phases of the incubation process.

5. Make absolutely certain you have a user experience (UX) expert involved at the inception of any software development process. Always remember that adoption is the metric of success; if users don't see the value in a solution, they won't use it.

Lessons from the Field

The incubation process wasn't theoretical—we used it to generate many practical and usable solutions. Two successful solutions that spring to mind are Brandwave and Express. Here are brief descriptions of each.

Brandwave was a solution for generating deeper levels of customer engagement and learning more about what customers wanted from a brand. We began developing it in the early 2000s, relying on available technology and systems. Basically, Brandwave enabled customers to snap photos of ads they saw on billboards or buses, send the photos to a database, and in return, receive coupons for the products in the ads.

For example, let's say you were the parent of newborn infant and you saw an ad for diapers on a passing bus. You would take a photo of the ad with your phone and send it to us in a text message. We would then arrange for the ad's sponsor to incentivize you with a discount coupon.

Nowadays, that might not seem like a big deal. But at the time, the cameras in mobile phones had low resolution and there were relatively few databases capable of handling the type of data we needed to collect, store, and analyze to create value for the sponsor.

Nevertheless, we incubated and developed a usable solution. By misfortune, another company had been developing a similar solution and beat us to the patent office. If not for that stroke of bad luck, I am convinced that Brandwave would have become a global standard for raising levels of customer engagement.

Express was born from our need to move very large digital files for advertising campaigns around the globe, quickly and efficiently. There were multiple drivers and reasons for creating Express, ranging from cost savings to client satisfaction.

On the cost side, we were spending millions annually to ship physical versions of the files by next-day air. We were certain that it would be much less expensive to send the files digitally, and our assumption was proven correct.

There were also problems with shipping highly time-sensitive materials by air. In many instances, "next-day" delivery can take three or four days, since shipping is highly dependent on time zones, weather, and other circumstances beyond your control. If a package misses its connection, it can sit in an airport until the next scheduled flight.

When time-sensitive materials are late, clients become unhappy and dissatisfied. Competition in the business is intense, and you always have to meet the client's deadlines.

So we were highly motivated to create a practical digital alternative that would lower overhead costs and keep our clients happy. In this case, we realized that we didn't have the resources or expertise to develop a solution internally. So we partnered with Accellion, a company with deep experience in developing tools for sharing and collaboration. That's when I met Nikhil Jhingan, who was Accellion's co-founder and chief technology officer.

Working closely with the Accellion team, we created a robust solution that met our technical needs, sharply reduced shipping costs, and improved relationships with our clients around the world.

The path to success, however, was bumpy and filled with unexpected challenges. We quickly discovered that the quality of Internet service varied greatly as you moved from one region of the world to another. In some markets, we had to develop and deploy additional hardware to make the system work properly. We also had to create versions of the solution in seven languages. In addition to technical challenges, we ran into cultural obstacles.

Eventually, we overcame the challenges and launched Express—only to encounter another unintended consequence. Express became popular more quickly than we had expected, and soon we had more users than we could accommodate. Initially, we struggled to keep up with usage.

After a slow start, the adoption rate was exponential within six months of the launch, which made us both proud and anxious. Fortunately, we were prepared to scale the solution, and we kept up with the high levels of demand.

The experience taught us an extremely important lesson: You can never just walk away from a new solution after launching it. You are responsible for the success of a solution even after you've deployed it. Like the original ideas from the incubator, the completed solutions you launch are indeed still very much like children—they require attention and hand-holding.

Net Takeaways

1. Continuous innovation requires formal processes; you cannot simply leave innovation to happenstance, or assume that it will occur naturally without encouragement and support.

2. Make sure to include the project management office (PMO) and user experience (UX) specialists in your incubation/innovation processes. Their participation is essential for creating solutions people will use.

3. Adoption is the key metric of success. Be prepared to manage problems and issues after a new solution is deployed; expect the unexpected and be ready to deal with unanticipated challenges.

Chapter 4

Operational Excellence

Executive Summary: In this chapter, we look at the fundamental relationship between operational excellence and customer satisfaction. We also introduce a three-tier model for developing solutions and services.

Operational Excellence and customer satisfaction are strongly related. Yet many organizations do not perceive the direct connection between the two. Instead, they treat customer satisfaction as an afterthought, something bolted on at the last minute.

The unvarnished truth, however, is that customer satisfaction is built on a solid foundation of operational Excellence. You simply cannot have the former without the latter.

In today's hypercompetitive markets, customer satisfaction is essential to long-term success. If you cannot deliver customer satisfaction, your days are numbered. This simple dictum applies to all organizations, whether they are large or small, global or local.

Even if you're running your business from a garage or a spare bedroom, your customers encompass a wide range of people and groups. In addition to external customers, you have employees, contractors, partners, suppliers, and other third parties. Somehow, you must figure out strategies and practices to keep all of them happy.

In a socially connected world, bad news travels with extraordinary speed. Your mistakes will stick to you like glue; make enough mistakes and your reputation may suffer irreparable damage.

Learning from Data

The strategic link between operational Excellence and customer satisfaction seems obvious, but I became aware of the connection early in my career almost accidentally while I was managing a project to unify our help desks.

Here's the story: in one of my first global roles, we began consolidating our help desks into a single support center. The consolidation was a major undertaking since we had help desks operating in a variety of countries.

As we unified the help desks and incorporated their applications and data into a central infrastructure, we observed patterns emerging. Let me take a step back and state categorically that I'm not the first executive to notice that help desk logs contain a lot of useful information. But most organizations don't have rigorous processes for capturing and analyzing help desk information. If processes are in place, they are often performed informally or haphazardly.

We decided to do it scientifically. Within a short span of time, we began reaping the benefits of our extra efforts. For example, we quickly observed that an enormous portion of calls to our support center involved telecom issues. When you're operating a global business with offices and clients all over the world, good communications aren't a luxury—they are absolutely essential. We also had another factor to consider: creative businesses don't work on a regular schedule so we had to consider a 24/7 operation in any given major city around the world.

If a fabulous idea for a new video campaign springs into your mind at 3 a.m., you need a reliable way to share the idea—potentially with visuals and music— with your team ASAP, wherever they are and no matter what time it is. That's how a creative business operates—the usual rules of "office hours" do not apply when you have a "Eureka" moment.

Moreover, we were a business based on significant deadlines. The branding and marketing campaigns we create are exquisitely perishable. If they arrive late, they are worthless. The first lesson you learn in creative business, as with most mission-critical businesses, is never miss your deadlines!

The data we gathered from our support center showed unequivocally that we faced a challenge of truly global proportions. To put it bluntly, many of our offices lacked the means for communicating information and exchanging data with the speed and reliability necessary to compete effectively in their markets.

Additionally, the cost of making calls or transmitting data while traveling was enormous. Remember, this was before the days when everyone had a mobile device. Back then, cellular service in many parts of the world was very expensive and spotty, at best. As one traveling executive said to me, "My hotel room costs less than what it costs for me to call my team in New York."

The support center data also pointed to a root cause. In many parts of the world, we were hamstrung by substandard telephone and Internet services. It quickly became apparent that we would have to devise our own solution to the problem.

Using the data from our support center, we made the business case for building our own virtual private network (VPN) to ensure our ability to communicate with each other and with our clients. A VPN works like a secure tunnel between devices; when you have a VPN, you don't have to rely on local telephone networks to make phone calls or exchange data. And because your communications are encrypted, you don't have to worry about unauthorized people listening in on your calls or stealing your data.

At the time we did this, the idea of a non-telecom company going ahead and building a VPN seemed far-fetched. But the data showed that we genuinely needed a solution to our communications problem, and a VPN was the best choice. So with the investment approval and good faith of senior management in our capabilities, we built one of the early corporate VPNs over the public Internet.

We launched our VPN in 2004, and carefully measured the results of our work, comparing the initial state with the current state. We were pleased, of course, to discover that calls to the support center about telecom issues dropped by more than 50%. Switching to a VPN eliminated 65,000 help desk tickets. That alone would have been cause for celebration.

The next finding, however, had a direct business impact. The cost of travel communications plunged by 70%. The savings from the initiative more than covered the cost of building the VPN and proved that there is rarely any return without an investment.

But here's the kicker: the VPN also allowed us to communicate more effectively with our clients and with the media outlets that published the work we created. The improved level of communication became a strategic competitive advantage for our company, enabling us to operate on a truly global network that our clients expected. It also helped us with fundamentals of disaster recovery. Many years after we had forgotten about the initiative, I was pleasantly surprised to hear that during hurricane Sandy that hit the U.S. East Coast, primary technology operations centers were successfully migrated to secondary centers in Germany in two hours, and over the network we built a decade earlier. The best part was to hear this from a client who said that a major European brand campaign was unaffected by the storm, even though it was developed in the United States and had to be transferred to Spain due to the weather crisis.

I love this story because it shows how a relatively simple effort to solve an operational problem at a very basic level can emerge as a strategic competitive advantage providing tangible benefits across the whole enterprise and its partner ecosystem.

The experience also taught me a valuable lesson and fundamentally changed the way I looked at the relationship between operational Excellence and customer satisfaction. It's easy to say that operational Excellence is a prerequisite for customer satisfaction. In reality, the relationship is a bit more complicated.

In other words, it's not a direct line. There are three levels or tiers in the relationship, and they must be approached in the proper order. You have to start at the bottom tier, which is the foundational technology. Then you work your way up to the solution, which is the second tier.

The third and topmost tier is the service you provide. That's where the rubber hits the road. Great service is the key to customer satisfaction, and you cannot fake great service. Our traveling executives didn't begin using the VPN because someone from headquarters sent them an email telling them to use it—they began using the VPN because it worked far better and was more cost effective than hotel services at the time.

We didn't solve the problem by starting at the top—we began at the bottom, at the foundational tier. And to be completely honest, the problem we solved was not the problem we set out to solve. Sometimes that's just the way innovation works.

Figure 4.1 is a very high level simplified three-tier model we developed for ensuring customer satisfaction. A quick glance at the model explains why enterprise-wide digital transformation cannot be purely top-down strategy. Unless you understand the foundational aspects of a problem, you cannot solve it with any degree of certainty. Maybe you will get lucky and find a solution, but chances are that you will become lost in a maze of complexity that leads to little progress on the CEO's change agenda.

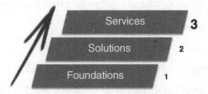

Figure 4.1 Bottom-up approach to service quality.

Earning Trust and Building Confidence

Working through the telecommunications problem also gave us the confidence and experience to tackle other foundational problems as they arose. Here's another example: one of our clients wasn't comfortable with the way we hosted its data on different parts of our network. The client insisted that we keep its data in one secure location and gave us one month to figure out a solution.

Building on the experience and knowledge we had accumulated while creating the VPN, we devised a plan to build our own private cloud for the client's data. This was back in 2005, years before private clouds became commonplace. In fact, we didn't even call our new project a cloud—we called it our "central infrastructure services co-location."

We built the capability and deployed it successfully. The client was happy, and we had a new arrow in our quiver. We measured the results and discovered that our cloud model was more secure and easier to maintain than some of our existing systems. As a result, we moved several of our overseas markets onto one centralized service, and saved substantially on operating costs by eliminating infrastructure spending in those markets.

As you can see, we weren't afraid to take a do-it-yourself approach in many instances. That said, I am not recommending a DIY approach for each and every project. You should still decide whether to "build or buy" on a case-by-case basis.

In the examples I mentioned, we benefitted from doing it ourselves because many of the now common technologies were nonexistent or nascent—we gained knowledge, experience, and confidence that proved invaluable over time. Additionally, we earned respect and trust.

Our internally developed projects also instilled a level of fearlessness that made it easier for us to move ahead quickly while others might hesitate. Many of the projects we've undertaken involve taking risks. No matter how many times you hear people talking about embracing failure, nobody likes to fail. Time and money are lost; sometimes reputations are damaged.

There's also the chance that if a project succeeds, it will make some technical jobs redundant or obsolete. I'm proud to say that our team never allowed those fears to stand in our way. Once we made the decision to move forward on a project, we acted as a unit, pushing ahead until we achieved our objectives.

Response Time vs. Resolution Time

Many companies judge the quality of their customer service operations by measuring how quickly they respond to complaints and close tickets. But that's a bad way to measure the quality of customer service and it can easily lead to trouble.

Any decent help desk can be trained to answer calls on the half-ring. Fast response times can be misleading, however.

The time it takes to respond to a problem is not the same as the time it takes to resolve a problem. Answering a call and resolving a caller's problem are not equivalent. In fact, they are very different activities. The wider the gap between the two, the more your reputation for customer service will suffer.

I had a painful learning experience with this phenomenon several years ago. I was visiting one of our offices in South America, and the CEO there was in the midst of pitching a major engagement to a large beverage company. While I was there, the office lost its network connection. The office manager called the support center. A ticket was opened and fairly soon the reason for the lost connection was discovered. A service team set to work on fixing the problem and the support center closed the primary ticket and transferred the issue to a different department.

Hours passed and the office still had no access to the network. The CEO knew I was in the building and he asked for an urgent meeting. He closed the door and asked me testily why the connection hadn't been restored.

I called the support center and was told the problem had been identified, and that a fix was underway with a different team. What the support center did not say, however, was that restoring the lost connection required a DNS (domain name server) reset. If you understand networking, you know that resetting a DNS can take hours or days in some cases. If you're the CEO, however, all you know is the support center said the problem had been resolved.

That unhappy incident taught me a highly valuable lesson: never confuse response time with resolution time. Sometimes the resolution follows the response swiftly. When it does not, however, you must be prepared to explain the cause for delay.

Better still, reexamine how you reward the people working in your support center. You have to do more than simply reward them for picking up the phone, listening to a customer, and closing a ticket. You need to reward them for resolving problems and following up to make sure the customer is satisfied with the resolution.

I included this story in the chapter because it underscores the relationship between operational Excellence and customer satisfaction. In this case, the foundational problem was the system of incentives that rewarded people for closing tickets. The solution was reviewing and revamping the incentives. The net result was improved customer satisfaction within the company, because the support center shifted its focus from offering quick responses to providing thorough resolutions.

Net Takeaways

1. Customer satisfaction depends on operational Excellence; operational excellence is a prerequisite for customer satisfaction.

(continued)

(*continued*)

2. Since customer satisfaction is an imperative in a socially connected world, the relationship between operations and customer service is strategic, not tactical.

3. Make sure that incentives are aligned to achieve customer satisfaction as an outcome.

Chapter 5

Customer-Driven Change

Executive Summary: Understanding the needs of your customers, whether they are internal or external to your organization, is absolutely critical to the success of any transformational strategy. It's imperative to remember that people will always be more important to the organization than technologies.

It took about six months for Alan Turing to crack the Enigma code during World War II. In the twentieth century he used electromechanical technology and arguably made one of the biggest contributions to the Allies winning the war. Fast-forward 80 years and it takes three to five years to complete a typical digital transformation. Why, despite all of our advantages and technological prowess, does it take us such a long time to achieve lasting change?

There are many stories about amazing people who overcame great odds in brief spans of time while under enormous stress. One of the reasons I chose this example is because it revolves around code breaking. Another reason, of course, is that Turing is widely acknowledged as a true pioneer of modern computing.

As technology leaders and executives, we often find ourselves in circumstances that are similar to those encountered by Turing. Time is short, resources are scarce, and the pressure to deliver results can feel overwhelming. We can be inspired by Turing, and we can also learn valuable lessons. Turing and his team had a clear task. That enabled them to set priorities and to follow through with precision at all levels of their endeavor.

So, what's gone wrong today? Forward-thinking companies transform to stay ahead of the curve and the needs of their customers but most transformations occur in response to external stimuli. Reasons for change range from threats to the existing business model to competitive environment changes, globalization, and disruptive technologies causing automation of the industry, but in almost all cases transformation is a reflection of changing customer demands. The importance of understanding the needs of our customers—no matter if those customers are internal or external—is paramount in the success of a transformation agenda. Understanding customer need is the single most urgent and most important starting point for driving strategy, setting priorities, and elevating operational performance.

Customer journey mapping can help establish the true vision of how a company wants to position itself to service the needs of a customer. Some journey mapping outcomes could lead to the creation of new lines of business, labor arbitrage, or even the transformation of existing lines of business; whatever the outcome, the bottom line is managing transformational complexity that can make or break the future of an organization.

Digital Alchemy

This digital evolution has steadily matured and led to the creation of online marketplaces, social platforms, and peer-review communities. It has led to the creation of supply chains, automation, and collaboration opportunities without borders. These developments have led to volumes of data gleaned from every customer touchpoint and used in everything from marketing to business decision-making. Collecting data in structured and unstructured forms to provide manageable information landscapes is a complex task, usually invisible and extremely technical.

This is where data science is indispensable. Quite frankly, if your organization does not embrace data science, I see little hope for long-term survivability or success.

We've all heard the term "boiling a frog," which refers to an imaginary frog placed in a pot of cold water. I've never really found evidence to the facts of this experiment but it makes for a good analogy in transformation. The experiment states that if the water is gradually heated to the boiling point, the frog doesn't realize the danger until it's too late.

From my perspective, organizations that are unwilling to disrupt themselves are like the frog in the pot—they realize the danger too late.

For practical examples of this phenomenon, just look into your wallet and then look at the apps on your smartphone. Almost everything you cherish in your wallet also exists in digital form on your smartphone. Your credit and debit cards, business contacts, membership cards, airline tickets, and even your cash—they're all converged on your phone, along with a web browser, GPS, calculator, camera, stopwatch, and dozens of other useful apps.

I use the term "digital alchemists" to describe organizations that understand and take advantage of this convergence. Here's an example of digital alchemy from an unlikely source: the United States Postal Service (USPS).

The USPS delivered 30 billion fewer pieces of mail in 2018 as compared to nine years prior. The ten-year trend shows a steady decrease in volume year over year and if not for newer partnerships and digital innovation, the USPS would not be able to show the $2.6 billion in increased revenue in 2018.

Today, the USPS prides itself on continuous innovation. For example, the USPS is conducting a pilot for self-driving trucks across state lines. This kind of experimentation seems a far cry from the early days of delivering mail by horseback, but it reflects the organization's earliest days, when the idea of national postal service was considered truly revolutionary.

Customer need also drives innovation in the retail industry, which is under margin pressures and often day trading for customers' attention online. Although early digital transformation efforts focused on supply chain optimization, the industry is now throwing its considerable influence into elevating and perfecting customer experience.

I would go so far as to argue that the industry's fixation on improving the customer experience has forced suppliers to provide higher quality goods and services, due primarily to the existence of online customer reviews.

Personally, I don't know anyone today who does not look at online customer reviews before buying a product or service. This effect is not limited to consumer goods; B2B technology companies such as Adobe have innovated aggressively to raise the bar, creating end-to-end experiences that are satisfying to users at every link of the value chain.

Smart companies also know they must provide excellent post-sales experiences, since unpleasant or unsatisfactory post-sales experiences can also generate negative reviews.

Automated Customer Services

When you call customer service these days, your initial contact may be with a chatbot or other form of automation. Chatbots can be a blessing or a curse, depending on how well they perform. Companies that devote the time and resources to deploying the best possible automation will reap the rewards; companies that try to skirt costs or rush their automation processes will struggle.

It's important to remember that we're still at a stage in which customer service is a blend of automated and human interactions. Again, the companies that take the time and spend the money to develop intelligent processes for escalating issues from chatbots to human agents will gain competitive advantages over the companies that take a slapdash approach.

Most of us will always remember a poor experience with a customer service center and we'll do almost anything to avoid using products or services from companies with poor customer service operations. However, we will happily spend our time and money with companies that treat us well when we have issues or questions. On a recent call with American Express, I was informed—to my pleasant surprise—that an electronic gadget that I had bought and accidentally damaged was covered by a warranty that I didn't even know existed.

Imagine my delight at discovering that American Express would refund the cost of the repair. To my mind, this is truly impressive customer service that makes me a loyal customer. I cannot say the same when trying to resolve a billing issue on one of my home services. Having been a customer for 11 years I was still transferred three times and lost 45 minutes on a call that did not resolve the issue. Needless to say the outcome of that call wasn't good for the service provider. We've all had these experiences and make "stay or go" decisions based on these experiences.

Smart organizations leverage digital platforms and improve customer service at all touchpoints, before and after the initial sale. But the future is constantly unfolding, with innovative products and services introduced continually. Today, virtually every new offering has the potential to compete in a global market.

A new digital environment is unfolding right before our eyes. Small, inexpensive sensors allow us to monitor anything from anywhere. With this preemptive model, a global equipment company can track the performance of its tractors on farms in Mexico, and issue warnings on which parts are most likely to fail, enabling farmers to fix their machines before they break.

In our homes, smart thermostats change the temperature when they detect the presence of humans (or pets) and smart doorbells alert us when there is suspicious activity going on in the neighborhood.

We are now experiencing a tidal wave of disruption that is both larger and more transformative than we could have imagined.

Basic Principles of Transformation

Digital transformation always starts with a well-grounded strategy. Yet it also requires a real understanding of three basic *C*s:

1. Change Management
2. Communication
3. Organizational Culture

Change Management

Transformational journeys are almost always difficult, for the simple reason that people do not like change. Over time, most people will adapt to change. But in the short term, change is frightening because it challenges the status quo. Although we enjoy complaining about our daily routines, we become comfortable with our routines because they make our lives easier. That's just the way it is. Always remember that when you ask people to change, you are asking them to make their lives more difficult for a period of time. There's just no way around this simple fact.

This is where many leaders and executives fail. Unless you've been through a transformation journey yourself, it is very difficult to understand what people are going through when they confront change.

Digital transformations are always about more than just technology. In most transformations, overcoming the technology challenge is the easy part!

The really hard part of digital transformation is changing the hearts and minds of everyone who will be affected by the transformation. Changing hearts and minds is the primary overarching challenge. If you don't get that part right, the transformation will fail—even if the technology works perfectly.

Communication

All change is ultimately personal. Anyone can change a table of organization on slideware. Changing the organization itself requires a deep set of interpersonal skills, beginning with empathy and the ability to communicate.

A good communications strategy straddles a fine line between saying too much and saying too little. You don't want to overwhelm people with more information than they need. But you don't want to keep them in the dark. The last thing you need during a transformation project is the emergence of a rumor mill that spreads false impressions, fuels confusion, and ratchets up anxiety levels.

I've found it's better to err on the side of too much information, but you need to be careful. Always remember that most people don't care about the technology itself—they care about how the technology will impact them.

That means you need to frame your communications in terms that people can relate to easily and understand at a glance. One email is not enough; ten emails are too many.

Ask and answer the all-important question for the affected community: "What's in it for me?"

I recommend testing your communications strategy on small focus groups. If there's one thing I've learned over my career as an executive, it's that in a time of stress and upheaval, a good focus group can be your best friend. If you don't know how to set up a focus group, ask one of your colleagues in marketing to assist or get professional support. It's easier than you think, and an excellent investment.

I recently spoke with a friend who is a top executive at a large global consulting firm. She reminded me that one of the firm's strategic goals is making sure that all employees are "digitally proficient" to the degree that they can handle virtually any client task assigned to them with contextual familiarity and minimum stress.

Stating and repeating this goal essentially puts managers on the alert, because they know they will be held responsible if their employees don't have the skills required for minimum digital proficiency as described by the firm. As a result, managers make sure their employees receive the additional training they often require to perform effectively.

It would be easy to say, "The company should do a better job of screening applicants and making absolutely certain they have all the skills required to function in a digital workplace," but in the real world, it's extremely difficult to assess someone's digital skills with any precision.

From my perspective, the firm's strategic decision to communicate its intent clearly and then cascade the responsibility on managers to make sure employees are properly trained is the right approach.

Culture

Ask a friend or colleague why they quit their last job and they probably won't say it was because of long hours or money. The most likely reason people leave jobs is because of poor managers or company culture. If there's something wrong with a company's culture, it will have a difficult time retaining top talent at every level of the organization.

For me, culture is virtually synonymous with motivation. I have worked on three continents and I have had many managers. Here is what I have discovered: when you have a good manager, you can get through the worst day and the deepest crisis. Somehow, you survive—not because of your own skill and talent, but because you know that someone in the chain of command understands your predicament and is watching your back.

Companies and organizations with great cultures attract great managers, and great managers tend to stay at companies with great cultures. That might not sound very scientific, but it is true.

Know Thyself

Adapting to the changing needs of customers requires adjusting to new ways of working. Assuming that your organization will voluntarily jump into a radical change is simply a misguided belief.

As mentioned previously, change is difficult; planning and forethought are requisites. Self-knowledge should be the first step of any transformation. With the idea of making your planning easier, here are four types of corporate cultures. Which one best describes your organization?

1. **Reactive:** Simply responding to a business stimulus that has already impacted an industry is not necessarily a bad thing; however, if an organization is constantly on the back foot, the chances of growth are certainly less than stellar. Reactive organizations don't retain great talent and find it hard to create a motivated workforce. Investments usually are the minimum required to catch up with the rest of industry. Large-scale transformations usually fail at these kinds of organizations.

2. **Adaptive:** Some organizations are great at adapting to the changes in their industry. They stay current without too much fuss and usually have an optimistic outlook to investment. They tend to be risk averse but are willing to take calculated investment risks. These organizations tend to handle transformation on an even keel but only if needed to sustain their survival.

3. **Dynamic:** Leaders in these organizations set the high bar and are focused on discovering big opportunities for growth. They create an atmosphere of innovation and are not afraid to take risks. They attract top talent, treat their employees well, and usually have happy shareholders. These organizations tend to be agile in their transformation journeys and achieve good results quickly.

4. **Visionary:** Leaders at visionary organizations go above and beyond. Instead of focusing on the doable, they strive for innovation and disruption. They are comfortable with transformation and perceive it as a net positive. Their employees tend to have heightened states of digital awareness and thrive in an atmosphere of creativity and continuous reinvention.

Real-World Examples and War Stories

I recollect joining a new team working for a CTO who had big, bold, and inspiring ideas. The team behind him, however, was focused on extremely operational tasks. While the CTO set his sights on the future, his team worried about deadlines, resources, budgets, and the viability of the new technologies that fascinated the CTO.

The CTO spent a year on the job but made little real progress. Then a set of external business factors hit the organization hard. The CTO moved on, taking much of his team with him. The new CTO dove right in. Amid the chaos, he saw opportunity. "Never waste a crisis," he said to me with a smile.

He quickly established minimum baselines and staked out a razor-sharp vision for the company's technology progress. His boldness and confidence were refreshing, despite the difficulties we faced.

The CTO's vision was unmistakably clear and firmly grounded in reality. So we went about our business of delivering on the targets he set. The bottom line: we hit our targets months ahead of schedule and the outcomes were better than we expected.

Reflecting on this incident a few years later, I cannot help but think that we would have been in a very different place and much better prepared for the changes in the market if the first CTO had been a better executive. Although he acted like a visionary, he was in fact a reactive leader. His inability to stay ahead of events was unfortunate, to say the least.

Here's another true story: I recently had the pleasure of speaking with a former divisional CIO of a Fortune 50 company in the industrial sector. She observed that driving change is hard, especially when people have been in their roles for a long time.

One of the challenges, she said, was that her team had been accustomed to working in a particular style. Their approach to solving problems was slow and steady. It produced incremental improvements, but it didn't create the kind of genuine advantages required to compete successfully in fast-moving markets.

She decided to shake up the staid culture of the organization by creating a series of internal competitions. She also looked for people who didn't quite fit the corporate mold—instead of hiring people who seemed "perfect," she hired rebels and iconoclasts.

Those small changes had large effects. Soon, the company wanted more. The team became more proactive and less conservative in its approach to solving problems and developing new solutions. New employees were encouraged to share their ideas more openly; it also created a level of healthy competition and tension and the team soon became a role model for the rest of the company.

I conclude this chapter with a keen observation from my friend, Vineet Jain, the founder and CEO of Egnyte, a secure content platform built specifically for business.

"We are fundamentally in the knowledge industry and our biggest asset is our people," Jain says. "Culture is not something you create. It is a collection of personalities, combined with a work ethic. It creates an environment that people would like to be a part of. The core ethos of our company is largely transparency: people knowing how the company is doing and what impact am I making or capable of making.

Transparency coupled with integrity is critical. It allows an individual to succeed or fail without the fear of intimidation."

Net Takeaways

1. Clear definitions of customer needs are essential for successful transformation projects.

2. Complexity in today's digital environment is a given, so clarity of purpose is more important than ever.

3. Change in behavior requires focusing strongly on human sentiment; the technology is important, but secondary.

4. Communications should be candid and relevant; include actionable steps whenever possible and keep people updated. Nobody likes being in the dark, especially during a transformation project.

5. Understanding your organization's culture will help you anticipate and manage challenges as they arise during transformational efforts.

Chapter 6

Strategy vs. Execution

Executive Summary: In this chapter, we unveil the five-step SPARQ process for planning and following through with strategic digital transformations. We also look at the execution challenges posed by matrix reporting structures in the modern decentralized enterprise.

In the movie *Groundhog Day*, Bill Murray's character is forced to repeat the same day over and over. At first, he feels that he is cursed and doomed. Gradually, however, he realizes that his entrapment is a blessing in disguise, because it gives him the chance to become a far better person than he was before.

This brings me to the first rule of strategy: the first 100 days must be repeated continuously. Moreover, you must continuously communicate the goals and objectives of your transformation strategy. You must communicate at a steady cadence to assure the message is getting through. That's the only way to guarantee lasting change in the business environment.

As a simple exercise, ask yourself when you last heard your organization's strategy stated or restated. If you haven't heard it in a while, your organization is drawing its inferences and deciphering the path for themselves. Lather, rinse, and repeat. Over and over. You simply cannot overstate the value of over-communicating.

A Blend of Science and Sentiment

Transformational change requires a special kind of leadership. Essentially, transformational leadership is a blend of science and sentiment.

Being a transformational leader isn't easy, especially if you haven't done it before. As with any new role, you will experience an early stage of apprehension, which is quite natural. The initial stage will be followed by periods of enthusiasm, excitement, discovery, ideation, creativity, and productivity.

The hardest aspect of this process is articulating the steps and imagining them as a path, rather than as a series of accidental events. This might sound obvious, but it's amazing how easy it is to surrender control and "just let things happen." When you're a transformational leader, simply allowing events to unfold is rarely a good practice.

Without being heavy-handed, you will need a structured plan linking actionable steps with tangible results. You will need to provide guidance and support. Your role in this process is not micromanagement—it is strategic leadership. You are the absolutely critical link between the C-suite and the operational world. In other words, your job is making transformation happen.

Setting Strategy

I find it extremely helpful to have a strong team of capable leaders around the table who will debate the pros and cons of ideas that I think may be good, but can usually be improved after a good discussion. These debates and conversations are also useful for separating operational concerns from strategy.

After the strategy has been articulated, it is crucial to establish checkpoints and test parameters to assess the viability of the strategy within the proposed business environment. Again, it is important to make sure that operational concerns do not infiltrate or dilute the strategy.

Here is a five-step process I use to aid my planning. I call it SPARQ, which stands for Structure, Partnerships, Accountability, Resources, and Quality.

Step 1: Structure

Before embarking on a transformational strategy, we need to determine whether we have the structure for achieving the goals we've set for ourselves. While this may seem like a natural enough starting point, it's a step that's often skipped over in the rush to get going. This is a bit like jumping into a swimming pool without first checking to see if it's filled with water.

By focusing on structure first, you will quickly discover which departments simply aren't ready. You might also discover that some of your offerings have become overly commoditized, your teams are not in the right geographical locations to support customer needs, reporting lines are too weak to withstand the strain of new demand, and too many direct reports in a single unit are putting undue stress on a good manager.

Speaking one-on-one with managers is a good way to begin, but it doesn't provide a deep insight into team dynamics. Sometimes social settings are more useful than formal meetings for observing the true dynamics of a situation.

Here's an example: I had recently taken on a new global role and was observing an afternoon workshop with a regional team. They knew I was there watching them, and naturally enough, everyone was on their best behavior.

At a dinner later that evening, I saw the team manager sitting apart from his group. He seemed isolated and distracted. I didn't think much of it at the time. But a few months later, as challenges in the region surfaced, I realized that I had observed an early warning sign. There were communications issues, missed project deadlines, interoffice politicking, and a steady loss of good talent.

It took a while to resolve the issues and to coach the manager. Eventually, we got the team back on track. I also learned a valuable lesson about the value and importance of team dynamics.

Step 2: Partnerships

Compared to transformational efforts in prior years, today's transformations require much less development by way of software or tools. Nowadays, most organizations lean toward the integration and leverage of reliable ecosystems available in the market.

It's important to remember that technology ecosystems are rarely designed and built in-house from the ground up. They are delivered and implemented by technology vendors and specifically from industry vertical specialists within the vendor organizations.

I'm talking here about presales, sales, engineering, customer support, and other parts of the typical modern technology vendor enterprise. All of those partners have their own goals, sales cycles, and personal aspirations for growth and success. They eventually become our professional partners; we call upon them regularly to support our own strategies.

The right partnerships will mutually inspire teams on both sides and deliver magical results in well-connected and supported ecosystems. The right partners will also make you the first port of call on pipeline innovation and potential joint customers.

Poor partner relationships can seriously hamper and slow down your efforts. Transformational leaders who don't take the time to develop good partner relationships soon find themselves at the end of the line, waiting for enhancements and improvements.

Partnerships have to be managed and a good people structure allows for that to be a priority that helps both organizations. As the old adage goes, a rising tide lifts all boats.

A personal example of relationship building for me happened quite by accident. As part of a technology transformation, my team had built an early partnership with a small technology vendor in Silicon Valley. We seemed to be making decent headway but not as quickly as I would have liked; then again, they were a small vendor at the time and we didn't expect them to have the resources we desired.

It so happened that their office in Germany were running a conference and a keynote speaker from the United States dropped out at the last minute. They reached out in desperation less than a week from the conference and we offered to have someone there to help them out.

Our presentation went off brilliantly, the audience was pleased, we gave our project lead some great exposure, and we saved their conference agenda. That simple act changed the relationship. From that point on, we were first in line and our projects always received top priority.

The simple gesture of helping a vendor build more trust and led to better outcomes for both companies. Based on that experience, we went on to create many successful partnerships with innovative companies around the world.

Step 3: Accountability

A digital transformation can be difficult even when you have the right people on the team. But a transformation can turn into a nightmare when the lines of accountability are blurred or poorly defined.

Matrix reporting is a case in point. Although matrix reporting is not uncommon in many organizations, it can be disastrous when executing a transformation strategy. I strongly recommend avoiding matrix reporting if at all possible, especially when you're tasked with leading a complicated digital transformation effort.

In the event that a matrix structure does exist in your organization, it is incumbent on the managers to jointly and clearly define and articulate the goals, stretch goals, and outcomes for the individuals reporting to two or more managers. It's not just important for the manager, it's important for everyone on the team to know where they stand in terms of accountability and performance.

In other words, people need to know precisely what they are expected to accomplish and when they are expected to accomplish it. Otherwise, everything falls apart.

Over the course of my career, I've worked for large organizations with matrix reporting structures. More than once, I've reported to managers located on different continents. Needless to say, these situations have been far from ideal.

However, you can't remake the world to your own liking and sometimes you just need to go with the flow. Your level of success as a transformational leader will depend to a certain degree on which type of matrix is in place at your organization.

Daryl Conner has written and co-authored several excellent books (*Managing at the Speed of Change*, *Leading at the Edge of Chaos*, and *Project Change Management*) on this general topic, and I find his model (summarized below) extremely useful when dealing with the inherent challenges of matrix organizations. Essentially, Conner describes three scenarios of accountability:

1. **Direct Accountability.** In a linear structure where the transformation leader sits between the business sponsor and the target group, this accountability model has the highest chance of success. The target groups are usually direct reports and the buck stops with the transformation leader.

2. **Lateral Accountability.** In a triangulated structure where the transformation leader and the transformation target group both report to the same business sponsor, the opportunity to succeed is much lower than in the first scenario.

3. **Indirect Accountability.** In a structure where the transformation leader reports to one business sponsor and the target group reports to another business sponsor, there is an extremely limited chance of success, since accountabilities will vary considerably.

As you might suspect, the third scenario is the worst possible matrix arrangement for enacting any kind of significant transformation strategy. It will present formidable obstacles, making it difficult to establish common goals and justify investments or spending reductions in areas you don't directly oversee.

For more insight and far deeper dive into the challenges of matrix reporting, I recommend reading Conner's excellent books.

Step 4: Resources

The heart of a successful team is the quality of the people on the team, the mix of good chemistry, and most definitely the right talent and skill to get the job done. Too many organizations lean toward the talent they know, rather than look for a fresh set of eyes outside their teams.

I too have been guilty of that. Early in my career, I overlooked meaningful contributions from a talented group of people simply because I didn't know them very well. They had developed a good solution and I didn't see its value. It takes a few hard lessons like that to overcome your apprehension and respect the diversity of your resource base.

Transformation work is not always fun. Sometimes it calls for significant patience and it definitely calls for listening skills. This can fray the most battle-hardened teams. But constant training, new challenges, a moderately competitive workplace, and a happy atmosphere will keep your people motivated and eager to be around each other.

Step 5: Quality

In the final analysis, the success of your efforts depends on the quality of your execution. If the product or output from the team is subpar or mediocre, nothing else matters.

Every aspect of the service you deliver must be measured against the most relevant parameters for your industry. In the service industry, for example, we typically use customer satisfaction, ease of use, response time, and consistent availability of services as our common metrics.

Whatever the service or product, you must ensure the right parameters are considered at the appropriate time. Be aware that the parameters will not be fixed or constant; they will evolve as the business environment around you changes.

Sometimes the changes will come unexpectedly. For example, several years ago we convened a meeting to discuss future tech investments with a client. In a stroke of bad luck, the Internet carrier was experiencing intermittent outages. There was nothing we could do but wait for the carrier to resolve the issues.

Our senior account executives, however, were furious. I vividly recall one executive asking me to explain how we could possibly expect the client to discuss future technology investments with us when basic services were unstable. I understood his frustration, and quickly activated fallback plans for working around our primary carriers. We then actively measured our ability to recover from even minor disaster scenarios.

Net Takeaways

1. Partnerships are essential; transformations are rarely accomplished without significant help and support from outside parties. Your ability to create and nurture durable partnerships will be a major determining factor as you move forward on a transformational journey.

2. Beware of matrix reporting structures; make sure that roles and responsibilities are clearly defined.

3. People are the engines of successful transformation. Good leaders find the right levels of personal

(continued)

(*continued*)

chemistry, training, talent, and motivation to keep their teams engaged and productive.

4. Measurement criteria must be designed upfront and be iterative throughout the transformation.

5. The transformation will only be judged on the quality of the results it produces.

Chapter 7

Hire Captains, Not Kings or Queens

Executive Summary: In previous chapters, we focused mostly on processes and technologies. In this chapter, we look at people—specifically, we share stories about finding and hiring people who thrive under pressure, enjoy pushing the envelope, and aren't fearful of the future and its uncertainties.

It's common for executives to complain about the difficulties of hiring top talent for critical roles in the modern enterprise. I agree completely—hiring talented people is difficult. But it's not impossible. David Ogilvy, often referred to as the Father of Advertising, the founder of Ogilvy & Mather, stated in no uncertain terms, "If each of us hires people who are smaller than we are, we shall become a company of dwarfs.

But if each of us hires people who are bigger than we are, we shall become a company of giants."

When parsing the difference between "difficult" and "impossible," I invoke the motto of the U.S. Army Corps of Engineers: "The difficult we do immediately. The impossible takes a little longer."

That said, I find it surprising when organizations erect unnecessary barriers that reduce the chances of hiring good people. For a long period of time, you couldn't get an interview at a major tech company unless you had attended a top-tier university and graduated with impeccable grades.

Some of the big tech firms have relaxed those high standards, but there's still a heavy dose of bias in the hiring process that eliminates many otherwise fine candidates. The CEO of a venture capital firm told me that he doesn't mind hiring college dropouts with passion to learn because education is not the only sign of a motivated team member. I agree with that philosophy because I've learned that you can teach skills, but you can't teach passion.

"Strategic discussions on digital transformation often focus on people, process, and technology; however," there are two elements about people that have to be addressed in order to make that statement realistic," says Sonia Fernandes, chief talent officer at Mediacom AsiaPac. "First, people are an asset.

They need to be nurtured, encouraged, trained, and managed. This cannot be an afterthought, it has to be a concerted effort because good talent begets good talent and vice versa."

The second element, she says, is managing employee feedback in an agile way. Being able to act upon employee sentiment—positive or negative—instills confidence in management.

"At Mediacom, we've adopted Amber, an artificial intelligence tool that allows for real-time tracking of employee sentiment. This allows managers to respond rapidly to situations that need attention. Daily dashboards and alerts help us synthesize large volumes of data and hone in on the most critical of issues with precision," Fernandes explains.

This chapter offers four real-life stories illustrating situations in which institutional or unconscious bias could have easily derailed opportunities for growth and development. It also demonstrates the value and importance of "captains"—men and women with the courage, tenacity, and wisdom to serve as leaders and mentors.

The Kid in the Corner

It's the mid-1990s. Eleven team members of a large global media company have been summoned to a meeting in India. The conference room is ornate, with dark wood paneling and frosted glass windows to ensure privacy.

The chairs of the team are arranged in a semicircle. A senior corporate executive with a grizzled beard stands inside the semicircle, describing a new technology that he says will change the world. He's talking about the Internet.

The team members shift uneasily in their seats. They're outside their comfort zone and not excited by what they're hearing. They don't want to hear a lecture from an older person who is potentially unfamiliar with modern technology that could change their lives. Some of the team members are visibly distracted and avoiding eye contact. They're hoping the meeting will end quickly.

In the corner of the conference room, an intern sits, quietly taking it all in. To the intern, the senior executive's words are spellbinding. In his mind, the intern sees a future filled with limitless opportunities.

The senior executive unveils a simple plan that will dramatically increase response times to global marketing campaigns and create enduring competitive advantages for the company and its clients. Essentially, he describes a globally connected digital economy with high-speed connectivity and the rapid exchange of information over secure networks—he was a decade ahead of his time and it was fascinating.

He speaks with authority and confidence but not having the desired impact on the team gathered there. Instead of embracing the senior executive's vision, they're looking at their watches and probably thinking about deadlines they had to meet.

The senior executive winds down his talk. He looks over the group of executives. He tells them he is looking for a volunteer, someone to help him choose and deploy the right technologies for attaining his vision of a digital future.

The group sits silently in their chairs. Realizing that he wasn't going to get any raised hands, he points to the intern sitting in the corner. "You," he says, "what do you think of all this?"

The intern realizes that he's on the spot. He hopes that no one notices his poorly made trousers, inexpensive shoes, and mismatched socks. The intern agrees, with little choice, to help the older executive achieve his plan.

I was the intern. The senior executive was R. Sridhar, head of the company's direct marketing operations in India. "You are my guy," Sridhar told me and went on to be my mentor for the next five years.

Sridhar became my coach, trainer, mentor, and champion. He showed me first-hand how to be a captain—the person who makes a genuine difference, finds the right talent, assembles a great team, drives the process, and gets the job done properly.

From Sridhar I learned how to manage people, run meetings, tell engaging stories, prioritize tasks, and keep projects on track. He included me in meetings with clients and senior managers. He brought me into regional projects and introduced me to global executives.

He showed me that captains provide inspiration, guidance, attention, and support. They work alongside their colleagues, not above them. He also taught me how to use nontraditional management methods such as yoga and meditation to manage stress and maintain focus. Most importantly, he taught me to view my career as a journey, not as a destination.

Years later, I asked him why he chose me that day. He smiled and said it wasn't an accident. He had already done his research and discovered that I was enthusiastic, energetic, and passionate about my work.

Sridhar wanted motivated people on his team. They didn't have to be the best or the brightest. He was willing to teach us the skills we needed to learn. We repaid his trust, and many of his protégés went on to become highly successful executives and business leaders.

We also continue learning from his example. When Sridhar recently asked me to critique an important new strategy he had developed, I realized that I was experiencing "reverse mentoring," which is when a senior executive seeks your advice and counsel. It was a wonderful and humbling moment that taught me another valuable lesson: captains learn and teach continuously. One day you are the teacher; the next day you are the student. It's a truly virtuous circle.

The Man with Blue Hair

Fast forward to 2006. I was now the company's global director of technology operations and we had been interviewing candidates for a major network security role. We were looking for someone with passion, curiosity, keen intelligence, and hands-on experience. Only a handful of applicants met our standards, and we were becoming anxious about our chances for hiring someone with the proper qualifications and the right temperament.

It was a beautiful fall day. My office was on the 15th floor of the Worldwide Plaza building in Manhattan. Looking out the north-facing window, I could see the sunlight reflecting off the newly built Hearst Tower in the distance. A helicopter was flying low over the Hudson River. Despite our anxiety, I was filled with optimism. We had narrowed the field and our network operations director had identified the best candidate for the job.

It is my habit to interview the final candidates for every major role in my organization, and I was looking forward to the interview. But when the network operations director walked into my office, he was frowning. Clearly, he was worried. I asked him to share his concerns with me, and he told me that all the preliminary interviews were done by phone, but when the candidate came in for the penultimate round, he was concerned that candidate might not "fit" the work environment. I told him that I would interview the candidate anyway.

At 3 p.m., the candidate was ushered into my office. For the purpose of this story, I'm calling him "Rob," to protect his identity. Rob walked in and sat down in front of my desk. He was wearing a hat, and I politely asked him to remove it while we spoke.

He refused, politely. "I'll leave it on if you don't mind," was his verbatim response. I like to think of myself as an easy-going type of person, but I wasn't happy with that response. Nevertheless, I wanted to interview him. Every previous interview with Rob had gone exceedingly well. The people on my team were impressed with his capabilities and expertise.

The hat, however, was irritating me. I wondered what he was trying to hide. I became distracted thinking about the hat. After a couple of minutes, I told him flatly that if he didn't take off his hat, I would terminate the interview.

Reluctantly, he removed his hat. I couldn't help but smile. His hair was bright blue above the hat line. I should explain at this point that I used to be a musician and had played in bands since I was a teenager. Extravagantly dyed hair does not shock me. Blue is just another color.

With the hat no longer an issue, we dove into a technical conversation about network security. It didn't take long for me to realize that Rob was incredibly well qualified. In fact, he was the perfect candidate. I was amazed to discover that he had built a small server farm in his basement, allowing him to experiment and explore in his free time.

At one point in our conversation, we began drawing schematics on my whiteboard. He removed his jacket, revealing colorful tattoos on both arms. By then, however, I frankly didn't care what he looked like. The job was his.

Looking back on that day, I realize how easy it would have been for me to yield to my prejudices. I'm glad that my better instincts prevailed. Rob stayed with us for seven years and became the leader of our network operations team. His knowledge, enthusiasm, and energy made him a wonderful colleague and great role model. Today, Rob holds a leadership role at a major network solutions company in California.

One of my mentors once told me that if you don't have at least one rebel on your team, you're probably out of touch with the latest developments in your field. I wouldn't exactly characterize Rob as a rebel, but he certainly was a unique and highly qualified individual who brought an unbiased outsider's perspective to our group.

The Receptionist

This story takes place about ten years ago. Jonathan, a brilliant entrepreneur, had sold his startup to a large marketing firm based in New York City. As part of the deal, Jonathan joined the firm and became part of its new digital business unit.

For a variety of reasons, the new unit was disbanded and Jonathan went looking for something else to do within the firm. He began pitching in wherever he could, and his talent for successfully managing complex projects was quickly spotted by the firm's senior executives. Jonathan was promoted to managing director and given a broad portfolio of responsibilities.

Once established in his new role, he discovered that many of the company's support staff had not fully mastered the use of basic office software. Their lack of proficiency and inability to handle simple requests slowed the pace of work and made it difficult to meet deadlines.

Jonathan knew that without a qualified support staff, he would be overwhelmed with minor tasks and would be unable to perform his duties as a managing director.

Then, on a particularly grueling afternoon, he noticed one of the receptionists leaving to take a break. Jonathan asked her if she had a minute to help him with a quick task, and she immediately agreed to pitch in. The receptionist's name was Liz. As it turned out, she had initially applied for a role in marketing, but had been turned down. When she heard there was an opening on the reception desk, she took the job.

Liz was highly competent. She knew how all the office systems worked and she had a keen appreciation of marketing strategy. But her skills and talent had been overlooked and she wasn't able to utilize her marketing talents while working on the reception desk.

It didn't take long for Jonathan to realize that Liz was precisely the kind of assistant he needed. At his request, Liz was immediately transferred to his unit and she quickly became a trusted member of the team. Over the years that followed, Jonathan provided both the support and the challenges Liz needed to achieve higher levels of success within the organization. As time passed, she took on larger and more strategic roles. Eventually, she became a managing director within the company.

Today, Liz is a globally respected and highly sought-after business consultant. She has also become a mentor and role model. Her rise from receptionist to world-class executive is truly inspiring.

Her career trajectory also highlights the critical role of captains in the corporate ecosystem. Jonathan needed help and he recognized her value. He wasn't afraid to walk into the human resources office, explain the urgency of the situation, and insist that Liz be assigned to his team ASAP. That's how captains change the world—when action is required, they do not hesitate. I've met and worked with both of these very successful people in the course of my career and know exactly what they're capable of.

Neha and Rahul

This story returns us to the mid-1990s. Neha was a senior manager at a large company in Bangalore. The company she worked for was in the midst of shifting from manual to digital operations, and the pressure on Neha's group was intense. As a result of the constant pressure, turnover in the company was quite high and good candidates were hard to find.

Neha needed to recruit a new assistant, and she had laid down stringent requirements to ensure that all candidates had the technical skills necessary for succeeding in the company's fast-paced environment.

The company also had unwritten rules that made her hiring task more difficult. Traditionally, assistants within that company were women. Few men applied to become assistants, and on the occasions where they did apply, they were rarely hired.

When Neha reviewed the test scores of the applicants, the candidate with the best skills was a young man named Rahul. Neha considered herself an open-minded person, but her initial meeting with Rahul did not go well. She was concerned by his lack of social skills, his extremely quiet manner of speaking, and his obvious discomfort with Western clothing.

But his test scores were impressive, and she decided to press on with his candidacy. Rahul was soft-spoken, almost to the point where Neha could not understand what he was saying. The essays he had written for his application exam, however, revealed deep intellectual capabilities and superior writing skills.

Neha asked Rahul to explain how he had become such a good writer. He told her that his father was an English teacher. At an early age, Rahul had been encouraged to read and study grammar. As a result, he had developed an extraordinary command of written prose.

Neha decide to hire Rahul. Despite his shyness, he became the team's go-to guy for writing complex business cases. People in the office would seek him out and ask him to correct and improve their writing. He earned the respect and friendship of his colleagues, becoming a key player on his team.

He also had a natural affinity for computers and he rapidly grasped the importance of business analytics, developing skills that made him even more valuable over time.

Soon after hiring Rahul, Neha left the company to start a family. When she returned a few years later, she found that Rahul had been elevated to a role on the analytics team. Today, he supports the company's wide-ranging analytics landscape, bringing consistency and rigor to complex processes.

When I spoke recently with Neha, she told me the lesson she learned from Rahul is not to judge a book by its cover. His introversion and discomfort hid his inner strength and competence. Fortunately, Neha was able to see past the superficialities. She opened a career path for Rahul, and he succeeded beyond everyone's expectations.

From my perspective, Neha is a true captain. She is some- one who can look deep into another person's personality and see the value there. Rahul wasn't a rocket scientist or a rock star. But thanks largely to Neha, he was a great hire and he became an exemplary team player in a highly demand- ing field.

Looking back over the course of my career, it seems clear to me now that captains play critical roles in the success of their organizations. Captains play alongside their teams. They show up. They inspire. They win together, they lose together. They share the glory, and they share the pain.

Captains accept accountability for the job at hand. They hire or seek out the best people for their team, often people they can learn from. They look after team members and make decisions that help the team move forward. They identify the areas that need improvement, providing encouragement and support along the way.

They have an intuitive ability to seize the moment and take swift action to achieve their goals. I know from first-hand experience that I would not have been on the wonderful jour- ney I've had so far without the support and guidance of a great captain. I'm certain that Rob, Liz, and Rahul have simi- lar feelings about the captains who played key roles in their development and success.

I'll leave you with this question: Are you hiring captains, or are you hiring kings and queens?

Net Takeaways

1. Tests and requirements are okay, but don't narrow the field of potential candidates by imposing strict rules that might eliminate people with critical skills.

2. Look beneath the surface when you interview candidates. Make sure the people you hire are truly passionate and committed to making a positive difference in the organization.

3. Take the time to coach, mentor, and support a variety of people in your organization. Sometimes the most valuable players aren't the rocket scientists or rock stars.

4. Don't be afraid of reverse mentoring. Even our least experienced employees can teach us valuable lessons.

5. You can teach skills, but you can't teach passion.

Chapter 8

Integrated Ecosystems

Executive Summary: In this chapter, we dive deeply into the challenges of real-world social collaboration in a global enterprise. We also discuss the enduring fundamental principles of collaboration and point to critical future trends that will aid your efforts.

When people hear the term "digital transformation," they tend to think of back-office processes such as inventory control, document management, invoice reconciliation, and payroll. Large organizations support thousands of back-office processes. Almost all of those processes are important to the organization in one way or another, even when they seem tedious and often bureaucratic.

But digital transformation involves more than automating or streamlining back-office operations; it involves the adoption of modern technologies that support every aspect of growth and efficiency within an organization. Over the course of my career one pivotal element stands out in early stages of the journey; I have seen first-hand that social collaboration is a prerequisite for digital transformation. Whether your organization is large or small, this type of platform absolutely essential to the success of any digital transformation strategy.

Without tackling the social collaboration piece first, your transformation efforts are likely to fail. Your plan might look good on paper, but it won't work in the real world unless you fully and completely understand the motivations, desires, needs, and habits of your users. You must understand what drives adoption. Without that understanding, your investments will not yield the desired outcomes.

It is astounding hear about companies spending vast sums of money on digital transformation projects without taking the first critical step of making sure that people won't reject the new digital tools and systems that are part of the transformation. If transformation were easy, we wouldn't spend so much time talking, writing, and worrying about it.

That said, we often spend too much time focused on the technology of transformation and not nearly enough time focused on the people who will make it happen. A major aspect of digital transformation is changing the way people think about their work.

It's critical to remember that people don't like change. As human beings, we prefer the tried and true. We like our routines and rituals. We prefer things that are familiar to us and we reject things that appear strange.

After all, it is quite natural for people to be suspicious of anything that is different and new. The aversion to novelty is hardwired into our human brains. It's a form of bias, and we need to be aware of it. Once we are aware of it, we can take the appropriate actions to overcome it.

Making the Case for Collaboration

From my perspective, social collaboration is both an enabler and an outcome of digital maturity. You need social collaboration to provide a strong foundation for your transformation strategy. After the transformation is underway it will gain credibility and gather momentum through the use of this very platform.

When a transformation is firmly established, it will provide a sturdy platform for productive collaboration across the enterprise. That's why I see collaboration as both an enabler and an outcome of digital transformation. In a properly equipped digital enterprise, collaboration creates its own virtuous feedback loop, continuously reinforcing and enhancing the value of your transformation strategy.

How does it accomplish this seemingly miraculous feat? Here are some of the ways in which social collaboration accelerates and reinforces digital transformation:

- **Enabling the sharing and debating of ideas.** Today, we work in cross-functional teams spread across multiple geographies. Social collaboration tends to erase boundaries and remove obstacles that impede workflow. It also makes it easier to share ideas that can lead to the development of new products and services. Collaboration is an essential part of lean and agile processes, allowing much faster cycles of prototyping, testing, refinement, and deployment.

- **Finding specialized skills within the organization.** People are constantly and continuously updating and broadening their range of skills. Looking for someone who is an expert in retail and speaks Thai? You can probably find someone in your company with the combination of skills you need—if your company has a social collaboration platform.

- **Managing through a crisis.** Our world is a turbulent place. A crisis can arise unexpectedly, anywhere on the globe. When bad things happen, the social collaboration platform becomes a place to communicate, reassemble teams, and respond effectively to the crisis.

- **Tracking workflow.** Whether you're building programs and projects for a client or for use within your organization, the collaboration platform offers an effective way for tracking workflow and analytics in real time, without having to wait for written or oral reports.

- **Disseminating case studies, success stories, lessons learned, and best practices.** Our successes and failures generate insight and information that can be shared internally. We have much to learn from each other, and the collaboration platform is a unifying force for sharing our knowledge and experience.

- **Training new employees in standard procedures.** It's hard to find your bearings in a new organization. Even the best training for new hires rarely covers all the bases. It's especially important for new employees to learn the SOPs—standard operating procedures. The collaboration platform can provide beneficial information quickly and effectively in a format that's informal and easily digestible for new hires.

- **Achieving global/local balance.** Every large enterprise needs a unified strategy, but the components of the strategy should be customized for individual markets. That means making certain that information is available in Western and in non-Western languages (e.g. Mandarin, French, Arabic) and in local dialects (e.g. Brazilian Portuguese, Mexican Spanish), as well as in formats that are accessible across multiple types of devices and networks.

The bullet points above represent only a fraction of the benefits that can be derived from a robust platform. In many companies, social collaboration has become the cornerstone of effective communications. It has moved from the fringe to the center of the modern enterprise.

Here's a hypothetical scenario illustrating the value of an enterprise social collaboration platform: let's say you work for a multi-sector technology vendor and you're meeting with a client. During the meeting, you uncover an opportunity to sell one of your company's cloud services.

This kind of situation occurs fairly often in the technology space. You're having a high-level conversation and suddenly an opportunity arises that requires specific knowledge and expertise.

This is when a collaboration platform can prove invaluable to the sales process. Immediately after the meeting, you click on your collaboration app and start searching for an SME (subject-matter expert) in the area of cloud services that sparked your client's interest. Next, you will reach out to a technical architect who can build a customized demo of the cloud solution that will address the client's specific need. You will also bring a pricing expert onto the team.

You will also alert your managers and keep them in the loop. If the opportunity involves a significant amount of money, you also will bring in an executive sponsor to meet with the client.

Apply this scenario to any type of B2B business and all of those players can be assembled internally through the collaboration platform. Additionally, the platform will be able to tell you which experts are available and where they are located.

Here's another hypothetical scenario: a client in the Middle East alerts you to a potential production issue in a certain system. The collaboration platform will help you identify and bring in the best available resources, in the nearest location, to deal with the issue as quickly as possible.

It's not an exaggeration to state that social collaboration has become essential to business everywhere. Collaboration is no longer a luxury; it is now an absolute necessity. It is also a path to leverage crowdsourcing opportunities.

Without these capabilities, vital information is trapped in silos and loses much of its potential value. Unlike tangible assets such as a precious metal or stone, information gains value when it is shared widely. That's one of the strongest arguments in favor of social collaboration: it increases the value of your information.

Don't Make Assumptions

Some organizations have an unfortunate tendency to assume that collaboration is a distinctly millennial trend. This is a mistaken assumption.

The urge to collaborate is a human characteristic. It's deeply woven into our DNA and it is a fundamental part of our lives as social beings. Humans have collaborated and worked together for millions of years. If there's a "secret sauce" that explains the success of the human species, that sauce is collaboration.

That's why it's important not to assume that collaboration is some kind of passing fad associated with a specific demographic or age cohort. If you build your collaboration strategy on an erroneous assumption, it will probably fail.

When Life Gives You Lemons...

I encountered a unique opportunity a few years ago. A corporate intranet in production was past its heyday and wasn't especially popular. With the goal of attracting a larger base of users the senior management wanted to revamp the ageing platform.

Technically, the project began as an upgrade. As the project progressed, however, the team gathered data from a base of potential users and realized that we had an opportunity to create something truly special. Eventually, an upgrade was deemed useless and a different approach to collaboration was required—one with the capabilities and strengths necessary to support a global enterprise. In effect, the new platform launched in 2014 was a sea change that brought us firmly and unequivocally into the social age.

Before embarking on the project, however, my team partnered with our corporate communications department to help us develop a deeper and more granular understanding of our community of users. The partnership with our communications team proved absolutely essential to the eventual success of our global collaboration platform.

The communications team surveyed company personnel in offices all over the world, conducting in-depth interviews with 120 people in all age groups and functional areas of the enterprise. Thanks to the survey, we had hard primary data on which to base our collaboration strategy going forward. The survey also gave us the confidence to dismiss our earlier prejudices about who would be mostly likely to use—or not to use—a collaboration platform.

Over time, we learned to define our social collaboration consumers by looking at three factors:

1. Geographical limitations of content distribution

2. Ease of user generated content submission

3. Ability to use personal tech within a secure environment

It is important to note that none of the three factors have anything to do with age or demography. Instead, they are contextual. We could sort users into groups by asking ourselves simple questions about their circumstances:

- Does their region have the infrastructure necessary to exchange high volumes of digital content?

- Are their networks robust, secure, and available?

- Can authorized users (employees, consultants, business partners, etc.) access and interact easily with the platform using their personal devices and technology?

As you can see, the factors were objective and easy to determine. They gave us a firm foundation on which to build what became our internal communications platform.

Through experimentation and testing, we refined and optimized the platform, eventually rolling it out to a large base of corporate users. Based on the insight collected from our survey, we divided users into three distinct communities:

1. Global

2. Regional

3. Local

Everyone who logged on to the platform landed on the Global Announcements and News Page, a page dedicated to worldwide communications and geography-based news updates. An algorithm we created looks up a user's profile and populates the page with relevant information based on their location.

Static navigation on the landing page enabled users to use a single sign-on (SSO) for accessing a host of tools and resources, including external syndicated research available to the organization, by using a federated system for sharing information from third-party sources.

Communities of Practice

A mission-critical aspect of the solution was its ability to separate groups of people into communities based on geography, customer accounts, and specialized departments and interests. Security between groups was of paramount importance.

To accomplish our goals, we divided users into three macro categories:

> **Category 1: Global Community.** This type of community could share everything with everyone within the company (excluding joint ventures (JVs) and affiliates).
>
> **Category 2: Limited Community.** The names of these communities or interest groups are visible to all but access to this type of community is predefined. One could request access based on need, but requests can be denied based on confidentiality.
>
> **Category 3: Hidden Communities.** These communities are invisible to everyone by default. Unless a person specifically has access, he/she does not know if this community exists. And the search engine limits this access as well.

Social and Collaboration Tools

Each business unit had the ability to configure their own navigation. This was based on a set of preconfigured guidelines but is driven by each independent business model. A given business unit had the ability to add in specific social tools as best fit their method of operation.

The social and collaboration tools available to each business unit/group were established through interviews and fell in line with most of the emerging industry platforms at the time and the fundamentals still hold true today, depending on the industry profile. They were as follows:

- Personal profile—edit and maintain current skills (required).

- Full form profile and skills search (required).

- Friend circle and personal wall for managing blog posts, reading lists, etc.

- Blogs/video blogs with content flagging capabilities.

- Wikis (how-tos).

- High-definition video training and archives.

- Threaded discussions.

- Manage team communications and subscriptions.

- Chat and online presence.

- Event-based news scheduling.

- Live Twitter feeds.

- Virtual drive—shared drive integration with collaborative editing.

- Digital publishing of PDFs and presentations so documents can be viewed online.

- Community calendars.

Innovation Targets

We felt we were breaking new ground and innovating in uncharted waters on many fronts as we progressed. But we had to gravitate away from all norms in three key areas:

1. Using social media appropriately within a professional organization. We were creating an advanced form of collaboration, taking full advantage of social behaviors to benefit our business, yet social media benefits are much harder to achieve and business benefits were much harder to measure in practical terms.

2. The contradiction of using open source to solve an intellectual property challenge. Open source offers a broad palette of capabilities, but it is very much like a blank canvas. Every day was a learning experience.

3. Collaborating with global resources to create global collaboration. Business requirements were gathered by speaking with 120 end users globally; the technology was sourced from a company in Silicon Valley, California; the architecture was done out of New York and North Carolina; the alpha test users were out of the UK; the development, QA, and testing were done out of New York, São Paulo, and Mumbai. Language integration and testing were done out of Germany and China. Creative design was done out of Singapore and implemented in New York.

Key Success Factors

It's easy to get excited about the technology; it's much harder to get users to adopt it and take advantage of what a system has to offer. We worked with the business units that had the most complex of all the requirements—from the alpha stage through beta, pilot, and launch phases.

Each of these sets of requirements were driven by the business CEO or senior-most leaders within the business units. This ensured that the end product was front-office ready for a global organization.

Great Execution Eats Strategy for Lunch!

Great execution is a mantra we try to practice within our teams each day, but this project set the bar even higher. After a shaky start, we scrapped the path of an upgrade to pursue a complete replacement of the system. This took some adjusting to in terms of resources, planning, project management, design, testing, information architecture, and user experience.

It took constant engagement with the business communities. Executing testing of even the alpha version across four continents was a massive undertaking that required skill and experience.

Lessons Learned on Execution

Unlike B2B applications, collaboration is more of a B2C solution with a wide range of demographics accessing the solution and many opinions on what works and what doesn't. Our lesson was that all organizations on a transformation journey will be measured by the quality of the execution, not the shiny slideware at the ideation stages, and this effort was no exception. Execution implies details, details, and more details: staying ahead of the issues as best as the team can, putting rigor into the quality governance process, testing and testing again, having meeting agendas, having meeting outcomes that are measurable, knowing what priorities meet the business goals for the initiative and what is "nice to have." This last part can be the death of a really good initiative. Trying for a perfect solution on Version 1.0 can work in some cases but is exponentially better if you operationalize it for a short period of time and then attempt to improve it. Voltaire said it best: "The best is the enemy of the good." And this holds true for scenarios like this.

Dealing with an Informed and Intelligent Audience

From the start this was a business-driven model with technology playing the key role with specialized capabilities and researching viable options. Some of the most interesting challenges out the gate were:

- The executive sponsorship team was extremely tech savvy and used to managing sophisticated online collaboration.

- Needs were based on the various online legacy communities that we had to make provisions for.

- Each business had diverse business models with less than 10% overlap across the six pilot groups.

- Another technology challenge was cost; the initial discussions on costs were during a recessionary period when the market was in a rather precarious position and we were looking to better manage technology costs. This caused us to settle on an open source technology, which had tremendous potential. However, every business requirement had to be clearly articulated and analyzed before the software came into play.

- Being a media company, design aspects were critical and had to be approved by the CEO and chief creative officer, who spent most of their time traveling to clients or our offices around the world.

After months of interviews, requirements documentation and sign-off, systems analysis, front-end design and redesign, information architecture, disaster recovery planning, staging, application fine-tuning, and user acceptance testing we had a global social intranet. It was a 360-degree turnaround from the legacy application it replaced.

The difference in philosophy, functionality, behavior, and acceptance is so vastly removed from the older application that the brand name, too, had been changed to reflect it.

Dealing with a Knowledgeable Audience

In most cases rapid prototyping helps stakeholders define the final outcomes of these types of solutions, but what happens when your stakeholders are extremely well informed and know exactly what they want? We encountered the latter, which made the challenge a little more daunting, as conversations often veered away from the business cases. Once we were able to harness that energy by capturing the stakeholders' needs, we were able to direct the technology to deliver the desired results. For practical reference, here is how one use case played out.

Global Research Use Case

Our company is in the business of brand building. Planning and research play major roles in the outcome of marketing plans and strategy around brand building for our clients and prospective clients.

The corporate planning department is spread out across many company locations globally, with the head of planning based in New York City. This team used traditional electronic communications within the group every day. Most of the communication was related to obtaining the right resource for the right client or business pitch. Often it was validation of results by specialists in the network.

The groups use vast amounts of research data and resources to come up with the fine-tuned results they deliver, and almost every department in the company uses them in some way. The sheer volume of communication, time zone complexity, and searches across these resources was an unsustainable process.

A briefing from the planning head in New York and the research lead in London clearly articulated the complexity of the global problem and the urgent need to find an all-encompassing system to address it.

We arrived at the optimal solution after months of working with the team on an extremely bold agenda that included high-definition video streaming, online training, document browsers, research material caches, case studies, reference material, suggested reading guides, global and local search, threaded discussion forums, and subsections such as global strategy.

The planning community was among the first to expose their capabilities, launching their strategy group from the collaboration platform in live demos to our global offices. The launch exceeded expectations and created a surge of enthusiasm, with around 500 planners adopting the platform in over 200 sites worldwide.

Here's what the worldwide head of planning had to say: "For the first time we are able to share syndicated research across the company. We can now allow hundreds of planners to create inquires and gather information from the various resources posted online. Overnight we have gone from a position where information could only be accessed by a handful of people, to sharing information globally. Large research investments centrally can now be leveraged across all markets."

More Lessons Learned: When Business Strategy Is the Only Driver of Transformation

We knew that technology was the answer to the problem, but certainly was not the place to start. We discovered that when tech is used in response to the complex business problem, we derived the most effective value from it. We also learned that

- Sponsors of the project must really want to solve a problem and not consider it a handoff to a CIO/CTO.

- Real feedback from potential customers of the platform requires "real and unbiased" legwork.

- Unlike proprietary tools that provide guiderails and case studies for business cases, open source software is a blank canvas and provides a plethora of options—the finished product is as good as the vision established at the start. This can be a blessing or a high-risk undertaking.

From those lessons, we realized that

- Technology platforms for social collaboration have come a long way in the five years since this program and one doesn't have to build any of its components from the ground up anymore. However, the principles of collaboration remain the same while the tools change with technology advancement. To name a few, tools like Slack, Trello, Egnyte, Workplace by Facebook, and so on integrate seamlessly and also allow for federated access across other proprietary platforms.

- The fundamentals on any social collaboration platform remain the same. Humans respond to the convenience of consumer-based technology (with appropriate data security) and these ready solutions achieve great traction due to a natural familiarity, which requires smaller changes in their behavior.

- In modern cloud-based environments, not only can an ecosystem of services achieve the same results faster, but they can also help you rapidly adapt to changes in your environment, by way of languages, scaling up or down, providing different dimensions of access for acquisitions, audit services, fraud detection, and much more.

Using Machine Learning to Solve the Information Overload Challenge

Within just a few years, collaboration platforms have improved significantly, but the ones that are emerging as the "future normal" are the handful that leverage artificial intelligence integrated within the DNA of the organization.

While early innovation around collaboration assumed that users of these platforms would flock to it and generate revolutionary ideas and content, we now have the problem in reverse: information overload. Medium- to large-sized companies in particular have this problem in more acute forms that are immediately apparent. "Search," which once provided rapid answers to queries, is now seen as an inefficient model that provides more information than one can coherently assimilate.

Consider this example. Even the most well-documented and religiously followed business processes are nonlinear (this is especially true for nonregulated industries).

This implies that exceptions are not solved by process alone but by tapping into the wealth of knowledge collectively possessed by the organization. But how does one approach the pockets of intelligence in the age of data and information overload?

Enter machine learning, a technique for teaching a system to recognize patterns of predictable behaviors.

The company with which I ran an experiment had a simple, yet powerful mechanism to manage business exceptions or complex queries. A simple illustration on the way it worked: a user posted a question to the general population or an individual. If somebody answered it, they received a rating related to keywords within that question. If they forwarded it to another person in the network who they believed had the better answer, that person was rated on whether they answered it or forwarded it on.

The answer could then be rated by other users within the network for things like accuracy, number of times the solution was successful for them, etc. Based on the number of positive ratings, the person who answered the question was rated higher, as related to keywords in the original question. The system gradually sees a pattern forming and starts to send queries to the "experts" based on best match.

Now consider the collaboration challenge in a multinational conglomerate with multiple locations and a multilingual and diverse workforce. The strategy and problem definition is exactly the same as a few years ago, but the approach needs to be far more responsive. In this case, the self-learning AI platform is effectively being trained by how the company responds to exceptions anyway, and over time, the "trained" system will begin to respond automatically as a recommendation engine. In this scenario, the knowledge sharing is integrated into the way the company behaves and is a powerful expression of AI.

There will always be instances where patterns are not well established and will not achieve the desired impact, which is why this is a low-risk solution whereby queries can still be directed to the experts by traditional methods.

The outcome of the experiment showed that over 24,000 queries were redirected to less than 5% of the experts in the organization. This statistic was true of the original collaboration tool as well, where the ideation and content was generated by around 5 to 7% of the organization, the key difference being that efficiency was hindered due to the huge volumes of information returned by search queries while the newer method was far more effective and exceeded expectations and response times.

The Future of Collaboration

Artificial intelligence may stutter a little while making its way into mainstream adoption. Also, organizations may be slow to respond to new technology that is not yet fully established, or even for the fear of the unknown. But in a low-risk use case like the above experiment, taking the mundane tasks out of the equation and making the organization more efficient is a great way to start.

Another trend that is quickly emerging is that of visual search; Google AI, IBM Watson, and Microsoft AI among others continue to make big strides in this area. A recent demonstration of Cloud AI capabilities shows significant development in the areas of machine learning, enabling one to search for matching digital images in a browser within just a few seconds. This capability will add tremendous value to keyless search (i.e. leveraging cameras, not keyboards). Combined with augmented reality and high-speed 5G networks of the near future, these technology combinations can leverage the fundamental principles of collaboration to achieve language-agnostic secure collaboration at scale without the performance barriers of just a few years ago.

This is the right direction for any industry that generates volumes of information that go untapped. It prevents re-creation, manages duplication, and expands your target audience while still ensuring governance to a centralized business strategy.

Net Takeaways

1. Social collaboration is critical to the success of all modern organizations, since it enables the organization to leverage the talent, skills, knowledge, and

(continued)

(*continued*)

experience of large numbers of people working together in near real time.

2. Developing and implementing social collaboration platforms require special attention to consumers of the platforms; they are unlike previous generations of large-scale software implementations such as ERP.

3. A successful social collaboration platform will generate, collect, and distribute enormous volumes of information. Harnessing this information will require various forms of artificial intelligence and machine learning.

4. Modern configurable platforms can help achieve this capability without the complexity of internal development.

Chapter 9

Digital Proficiency and Innovation

Executive Summary: Even though advanced technology has become a commodity, organizations still need to develop the mindset required for using technology wisely and effectively. I call this mindset "digital proficiency," and from my perspective it's more essential to success than technical proficiency.

The Apollo 11 spacecraft that took men to the Moon in 1969 relied on a guidance computer that could handle eight jobs at a time. Today, an iPhone can theoretically process 6 billion transactions per second.

We've come a long way since the days of the Apollo program. Thanks to the spirit of human invention and Moore's

Law, amazing technologies have become commoditized and commonplace. In our modern techno-savvy culture, virtually every organization can craft a practical business solution with technologies that are readily available at a reasonable cost.

In other words, technical proficiency has become a given. What is not a given, however, is digital proficiency. For most organizations, the widespread lack of digital proficiency remains a barrier to transformation.

Why is this so? The answer is maddeningly simple: to achieve their goals and objectives, organizations typically rely on the skills and knowledge of their employees. That makes sense, doesn't it? After all, that's the reason you hire people, so you can leverage their skills and knowledge.

But here's the rub: the typical employee relies on skills and knowledge that he or she learned years ago in school. That's the problem! Unlike riding a bike or driving a car, digital skills require continual upgrading. The need for continual learning and development is not some trivial matter. Ignoring the "skill state" of your workforce can prove disastrous.

Today, acquiring new digital skills almost always entails more than merely learning how to use a new piece of software or supervise new business processes. Many of the newer solutions require users to adopt a new mindset and a new approach to work. Many newer solutions aren't merely new—they are disruptively new, requiring users to become familiar with a newer dictionary and new terminologies.

Again, these aren't trivial problems. And they are compounded by vast differences in levels of preparedness and experience across the modern workforce. In today's workplace, one size definitely does not fit all. "For the first time in our history we have four generations working side by side," says Mitra Best, lead principal of strategic innovation and technology at PwC.

Please take a moment to consider her observation. The idea of a multigenerational workforce isn't new, but I cannot remember a time when four generations of employees worked together. The impact of the multigenerational workplace is powerful and undeniable.

Yet most organizations are constantly operating in beta mode when it comes to training. A handful of large corporations take learning and development seriously, but midsize companies are still way behind the curve. Small companies and startups often focus on hiring people with great technical skills, but fail to hire digitally proficient talent in critical areas such as sales, marketing, finance, and human resources.

What's the net effect? There are gross imbalances in levels of proficiency, not just across companies, but across departments and teams as well. These imbalances can have dire consequences for transformational strategies in modern organizations.

How often have you heard technologists use the phrase "Build it and they will come," but invariably the platform investments fall short, or worse still, completely miss the desired objective. Even though technologists form an integral part of a transformation, the keen sense to research solutions without adequate definition of the business challenge is a very slippery slope. While it is imperative to identify the business-oriented components of any transformation prior to identifying supporting technologies, most programs repeatedly fall into the same trap of not doing so with rigor. If you look at the SMART transformation approach shown in Figure 9.1, I've drawn up a simple method on how to approach this challenge by drawing on commonly used business practices to aid the journey.

The acronym identifies the five steps that one can follow while interchanging the underpinning steps to suit the challenge. Consider it a prequel or a step in the journey leading to the actual transformation.

Survey. The first step in the journey is defined to indicate inclusion of the various stakeholders. In most transformational cases there is already a method to achieve the business goals, so before disrupting established methods it is crucial to understand what is in place and if it does indeed need to be changed.

Map. A simple process within an organization may have multiple stakeholders from commercial teams to supply chain personnel in different geographies. I find that visually mapping this process brings about the reality of how complex things really are under the

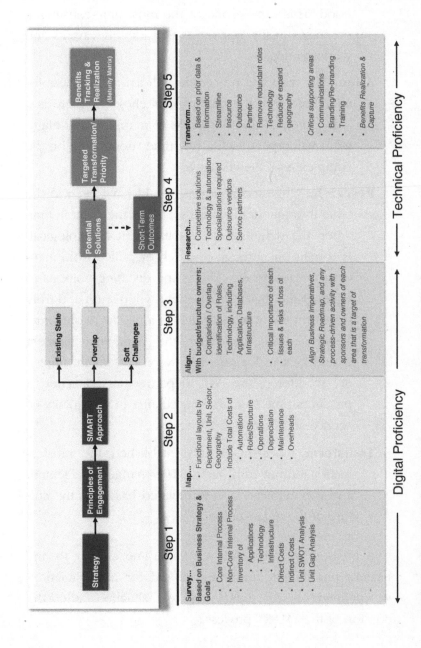

Figure 9.1 The SMART business and digital transformation method.

129

hood. This can be one of the most time-consuming processes in the journey as you identify caveats and workarounds.

Align. The mapping procedure will act as the basis for alignment with the multiple stakeholders; there is a high potential that this cycle of mapping and alignment will repeat itself a few times depending on the complexity of the challenge.

Research. While technologists would have been at the table throughout this process, this is the point in time when the definition of a solution, if technological, is sought out through research or pulled from incubators, startups, etc. This is the deciding point as to whether the digital enablement will disrupt and truly transform the process or deliver a mediocre outcome. This is also the point where the change management would kick in for how a new process might impact the workforce, the P&L, departmental efficiency, a product's time to market, a change in the quality of service, etc.

Transform. Once this is fully established, the transformation journey truly begins. The change management and communication is formulated based on the culture of the organization.

No method will give you a straight-line answer to any business problem; it must be adapted for each situation. I've outlined one of these very real situations after the adoption of the SMART process.

Here Come the Robots

Robotics offers a good example of the disparities in knowledge that are typical in the modern workplace. Robotics is a multidisciplinary field and there is no standard "robot." Robotics includes physical robots, AI chatbots, autonomous driving systems, and RPA, which is the abbreviation for robotic process automation. Despite the variety and diversity of robotics itself, the idea of robots inspires two unpleasant thoughts in the minds of many people:

1. They are taking over the world.

2. They are eliminating my job.

Most people don't have a clue about what robotics can and cannot do. Why is that a problem? It's a problem because the chances are very good that your next digital transformation project will involve some degree of robotic process automation. Simply hearing the word "robotic" will sow seeds of fear and panic among your workforce, making your role as agent of transformational change even more difficult.

From my perspective, the ability to talk about newer technologies such as robotics is a critical aspect of digital proficiency. In other words, digital proficiency isn't just about knowledge and skill—it's also about explaining why and how things work in the modern workplace.

The CEO of a digital marketing agency recently shared his frustration over the inability of a key team to explain the value proposition of a new technology platform they had developed for an important client.

I found the conversation fascinating. At no point did the CEO mention any problems with the technology involved in the project. The technology was great, he said. His sole issue was the team's inability to articulate the technology's value proposition to the client.

A Long and Winding Road

Business requirements and organizational needs drive digital transformation. And since every business and every organization is different, the term *digital transformation* has no strict definition. It varies by industry and by company. But there are common threads that can be woven into a coherent story. Recognizing these threads and weaving them together is part of digital proficiency.

A transformation leader recently told me a story that underscores this point. The leader's company was experiencing persistent problems with its customer invoicing processes. There were constant delays, inaccuracies, and complaints from irate customers. Eventually, the problems were traced to deeper issues in a back-office function. Additional training didn't help, and there were no pragmatic solutions for reorganizing the back office.

A deep analysis of the data indicated that about 70% of the back-office work was mostly computational and about 30%

was complex enough to require human cognition to process. This seemed like a natural opportunity for deploying a simple robotic processing automation solution.

But the decision to use RPA was only the beginning of a longer journey. The leader identified seven distinct stages in the journey and outlined them for me:

Stage 1: Outright Rejection. The back-office unit initially rejected the idea of automation. Employees in the unit pushed back hard, saying that automation was a far-flung idea, not ready for primetime, untested, too technical, and would never pass an audit. They complained that it would cost too much, would clash with existing scripts and automation, and would not work on older versions of their existing software platform.

Stage 2: Fearful Acceptance. Although the analysis indicated that 70% of the work was computational, the employees thought the figure was inaccurate. They also feared for their jobs. The leader responded by assuring them that they would be retrained and reallocated to another department if their jobs were eliminated by automation. Gradually, however, they accepted the idea that automation was coming.

Stage 3: Alignment of Processes. While the back-office unit had well-established processes which should have made the transformation easier, the employees had made minor nonconforming changes over time.

As a result, the entire process had to be re-mapped and realigned before it could be programmed into bots.

Stage 4: Buy-In. The leader had expected that she would get buy-in from the company's technology group. But her expectations didn't match up with reality. The technology group wasn't aligned with the business strategy and had its own plans for automating processes across the company; the back-office RPA project was not on its roadmap. It took months of negotiating with the technology group to reach an accommodation that addressed the back-office issues without undermining the company's long-range strategies.

Stage 5: Audit Engagement. Before the test launch, the company's internal audit team had to review the naming convention used by the unit to designate the RPA bots. This seemed like a simple step until a team of external auditors deemed the process a "material change" of the organization's end-to-end workflow. It took weeks to assure the auditors that humans were still in the loop and overseeing the bots to guarantee the accuracy of their work.

Stage 6: HR Concerns. After clearing many hurdles, another barrier remained: corporate governance required adding the bots to the company's HR database. This might seem humorous, but the HR team was flummoxed since it had never handled a request like this before. Again, weeks were lost as new processes were negotiated and approved.

Additionally, since the HR database required human names, exceptions were necessary to include the bots, which were identified by numbers rather than names.

Stage 7: Determining Employment Status of Bots. Again, it might seem strange to discuss the employment status of a bot, but the company's procurement organization raised the question, leading to a long and difficult conversation about the nature of robotic assistants and other forms of automata. Eventually, a licensing system was devised to get around the thorny issue of whether bots should be treated as workers or as machines.

This story represents only the tip of a much larger iceberg. While the leader felt as though she was in a unique situation, the truth is that scenarios like this will become increasingly common as companies integrate automation into their normal workflows. The questions and issues raised during the transformation process were far from trivial. Echoing the words of the auditors, the changes were "material," and they needed to be treated with the utmost gravity.

It's a cop-out to label every business transformation as a digital transformation. The real transformation must occur within the hearts and minds of the people involved.

Innovation and the Agility Paradox

A lack of digital proficiency in an organization will lead to a drop-off in nontraditional problem solving. The most successful consulting organizations require a minimum digital proficiency training that is not just a "talking point" but is formally measured and managed. Organizations that streamline these approaches to proficiency tend to lead the pack in forward-thinking and innovation.

Net Takeaways

1. Technical proficiency is not the same as digital proficiency.

2. Make no assumptions as to the level of understanding of departments involved in a digital transformation undertaking.

3. Infrastructure is in an advanced and commoditized state and should be a peripheral consideration.

4. Digital transformation involves more than installing new technologies; there are social and moral issues to consider as well.

5. Digital proficiency leads to more innovative problem solving.

6. The pace of change tomorrow will be faster than it is today.

Chapter 10

Are You "Digitally Determined" or "Digitally Distraught"?

Executive Summary: Digital transformation requires more than grit, tenacity, and optimism. You need a single strategy to guide the multiple components of transformation in a holistic and coherent manner across the enterprise. A transformational strategy must be your North Star across the enterprise; transformations that are limited to lines of business or functional areas of the organization are unlikely to deliver the desired results.

A recent memorial honoring the armed forces on the 75th anniversary of D-Day brought to mind the tremendous ingenuity of the Allied forces. Their creativity, imagination, and willingness to innovate changed the course of World War II.

They were truly brilliant and fearless in their approach. Many paid the ultimate price, yet they will be long remembered for their struggle to liberate a continent and restore freedom to millions of people.

I visited the WWII museum in New Orleans not too long ago, and reflected on the terrible paradox of war, which brings out the worst and the best in humanity. Focusing on the best of outcomes, the war motivated people to innovate in thousands of ways, both big and small. From their efforts sprang better antibiotics, advanced forms of surgery, pressurized aircraft cabins, microwave ovens, and practical electronic computers. Their innovation launched an economic revolution that changed the world.

Seventy-five years later we are seeing a similar drive to innovation. It is important to note that digital innovation is not new. The early stages of the digital revolution are sometimes referred to as the "Third Industrial Revolution" and the current phase, which includes the rise of practical artificial intelligence, is sometimes called the "Fourth Industrial Revolution." Whatever you call it, the names are less significant than the effect.

I prefer to think of the current digital revolution as a kind of renaissance because the technological maturity we've achieved has now greatly accelerated the speed at which industries are able to innovate.

This renaissance is driving massive change in every imaginable corner of the global economy. Every traditional industry is experiencing some form of disruption caused by the application of newer technologies.

Disruption has always been at the heart of progress, but the pace of change today is creating a special problem that I call the "agility paradox." Here is the paradox in brief: new companies have little or no legacy system to manage, so they can respond much more rapidly to changes in the surrounding environment than incumbents, who are burdened by their legacy systems.

Newer organizations allow digital technologies to permeate and influence every aspect of their working ethos while traditional organizations tend to maintain the institutional culture that brought them to prominence.

For example, I've heard top executives at many traditional organizations pay lip service to concepts such as design thinking, even when it's clear they have no idea what design thinking is or how it works.

Yet when I speak with startup founders and their teams, it's clear that they understand the critical importance of design thinking and have woven its basic principles into the fabric of their organizational culture.

Design thinking has become such an integral part of their lives that they just do it subconsciously. It's second nature to them, which explains why they can stay in sync with their customers and users. Design thinking goes a long way toward explaining why startups always seem nimbler than incumbents.

Traditional organizations excel at running the major operational components of their businesses. In fact, that's their core competency. Operational expediency is crucial to long-term success; that is inarguable.

Why Digital Transformation Seems Confusing

Ask a group of ten business leaders to define digital transformation and you will get 12 different answers—and none will be wrong. Here's why: digital transformation is a wraparound term used to signify a process that defies easy description. It's an intentionally amorphous term whose meaning shifts and changes depending on the context in which it is applied.

Although the term itself is abstract and general, each and every instance of digital transformation is concrete and specific. Talking or writing about digital transformation does not equal doing digital transformation. It's like buying a home or starting a family. It's one thing to plan a life-changing event; it's quite another thing to actually do it.

The overarching purpose of this book is to remove some of the confusion surrounding digital transformation. My goal is demystifying and clarifying a process that is inherently dense and complicated. (See Figure 10.1.)

Fixating on operational efficiency alone creates a legion of unseen costs and burdens that can adversely impact profitability. It's essential to remember that operational efficiency

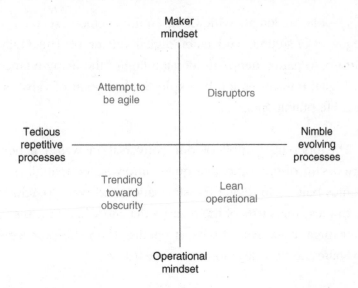

Figure 10.1 Perception and Truth matrix.

isn't free. Achieving efficiency is expensive, a fact which is often overlooked or forgotten.

Agile organizations as a general rule tend to buy services from specialized service providers and focus on their core business. This also allows for predictable costs based on growth. Scaling up or down is contractually managed rather than becoming an administrative overhead. BPO and Software as a Service (SaaS) are varying examples of this.

Agent of Change

Ever wonder why the term *digital transformation* has so many definitions and why each definition is slightly different? The cause of confusion is simple: digital transformation means different things to different businesses.

I spoke at length with Carla Hendra, chief executive of Ogilvy Consulting, and chief digital officer of The Ogilvy Group, to gain a deeper understanding of the many nuances of digital transformation by exploring her point of view as a real-life practitioner.

The opening gambit of our conversation was a general discussion of the topic. She quite simply stated that all companies believe in digital transformation and want to achieve it, but less than 10% of them can articulate what it means for their organizations and what it entails. Then she proceeded to share the best description I've heard yet.

"We define digital transformation simply as establishing new pathways to growth that take advantage of all the new possibilities in technology. And even as technology changes every day and impacts a variety of industries in the B2B or B2C, in all cases the customer journey must map to a new and better customer experience."

Using this simple definition of growth-focused digital transformation means leveraging mature technology in the service of a business. That means digital transformation can serve a wide variety of desirable outcomes, such as expanding a portfolio of competitive products, opening new markets, creating a better planet, or simply improving financial margins.

Merely formulating a digital transformation strategy isn't enough. You also need to communicate the strategy and translate it into a set of actionable plans and measurable outcomes. From her own experiences, Hendra says that successful strategies include long-term technology transformation, digital transformation, and customer experience transformation. Great organizations, she says, focus on creating customer loyalty and trust.

Three Fundamental Objectives

In today's digitally connected world, most organizations strive for three fundamental objectives:

1. Better conversations
2. Faster transactions
3. Precise information

Competitive businesses also strive intensely to keep pace with the rising technology curve. The most successful organizations (e.g. Apple, Amazon, Google, Facebook, and Netflix) anticipate the rise of new technologies and leverage them to create innovative products and services that enable them to leap far ahead of their nearest competitors. From my perspective, this is the heart and soul of digital transformation: the ability to anticipate and deploy new technology faster and better than your competitors.

Let's take a brief look at the recent evolution of digital transformation. It began with electronic data processing on a limited network. This in turn led to "islands of automation," which we consolidated and built into data centers.

The sprawling infrastructure that followed went through its own evolutionary period of consolidation and then for the first time we stepped away from core infrastructure offerings to a realm that included capabilities such as business process management, total quality management, and business process reengineering. Eventually, the complex and expensive platforms built to support those earlier capabilities evolved into platforms that were more modular and more affordable, setting the stage for the era of continuous digital transformation we are experiencing today.

It's true that technology moves at a rapid pace and it seems that the principle behind Moore's law can now be extended to every aspect of digital transformation, which is why it may seem monumental when looked at holistically. In many respects, digital transformation is the newest incarnation in the never-ending quest for competitive advantage. That's why people often use the terms "digital transformation" and "business transformation" interchangeably, which only adds to the general sense of confusion.

Better Conversations

In the past, digital evolution relied heavily on prior investments and the foundations of coding, infrastructure, and data centers. Today's incarnation of digital evolution relies very little on legacy solutions.

It's almost as if there has been a change in our DNA, a shift in our approach to solving business problems. Today, our emphasis is not on making the LEGO blocks themselves; instead, we're focused on putting the blocks together to create the infrastructure we need to deliver value.

We've gone from building systems to creating digital experiences; from constructing data centers to creating on-demand infrastructure; from architecting networks to plugging into the web; and from setting up firewalls to sophisticated cybersecurity practices.

Yesterday		Today
Building systems	=>	Creating digital experiences
Constructing data centers	=>	Creating on-demand infrastructure
Architecting networks	=>	Plugging into the Internet
Configuring firewalls	=>	Zero-trust cybersecurity strategies

Most importantly, we're enabling the business to move far beyond traditional sales and marketing strategies. Instead of helping the company search for customers, we're helping customers find us. We're setting up digital ecosystems, enabling us to meet and interact with our customers where they live, work, and relax. Sometimes our customers are in physical locations and sometimes they're on web browsers or their mobile apps. No matter where they are, digital transformation enables you to reach out and interact with them.

Faster Transactions

The output from a digital ecosystem is data, not information.

Now that we are creating environments for our customers to digitally interact with us, enabling the fastest possible transactions, these vast volumes of data need to be able to tell a story, shape the conversation, provide management with indicative trends, improve the supply chain, make decisions on investments, and so on.

But this poses its own set of challenges; unlike the digital marketing world where data volumes are large and complex and the fragmentation from multiple social channels is mind numbing, for the most part organized digital ecosystems that companies are now maturing to churn out more structured data, not information.

That's up to the quality of analytics that we can churn out and is no small feat. Moreover, this information that is culled from the data needs to be in near real-time or instantaneous depending on the business. This calls for a different type of compute and certainly more precise information.

To consider the future of these complex ecosystems, one case in particular makes for an interesting example—a smart city ecosystem. IoT sensors will most likely be built into everything from traffic light triggers, to lane keeping mechanisms, e-commerce from a moving connected vehicle, speed tracking built into street lights, pedestrian heat tracking sensors in cars, autonomous vehicles, electric vehicle charging stations, smart keys, vehicle remote control apps, and various other safety features.

The data output from these various sources needs to come together rapidly and often quite simply either to elicit an immediate response from a driver or for guidance to a vehicle to take immediate action. This would be similar to airline anti-collision technology but at a much higher rate of transmission due to the volume of vehicles in close proximity.

Precise Information

I recently sat down with a lead engineer dealing with complex unstructured data sets from e-commerce channels and the biggest challenge that team faced was the lack of standards among the various sources. The engineers on that team spent 70% of their time ensuring that the data sets could be joined up in some meaningful way. Then they spent the rest of the time running analytical algorithms on the data. Unfortunately, this challenge is more common than one would assume. While faster transactions give the aura of high performance and accuracy, the true value is in deciphering the data at a rapid pace.

Here's where machine learning and pattern matching can be highly useful. Often grouped under the general heading of artificial intelligence, they are practical methods for using raw compute power to find data patterns that can deliver macro results, discover anomalies, and pinpoint hidden issues.

Machine learning and pattern matching methods aren't magical, however. Both depend on algorithms, which are step-by-step processes written by people and used by computers for processing data. Typically, algorithms need time to "understand" the data they're handling. The more data you feed them, the more they will learn. After an initial period of learning, the algorithms can dramatically shorten the span of time required to arrive at the goal of information precision.

The engineering team I mentioned earlier implemented a machine learning layer on top of the unstructured data set and established data joins in under an hour, an achievement that would have been impossible just a few years ago due to the volume and complexity of the data. The information derived from their efforts helped their client gain new insights and compete more effectively in a crowded market.

Key Strategic Elements and Success Factors

Assume nothing. That's a lesson I've learned first-hand over my career. For instance, it would be easy to assume that a successful transformation strategy depends largely on having a good set of ground rules. While ground rules are important, they are not sufficient to guarantee a positive outcome.

While I've always known this, my conversation with Hendra, president of Ogilvy Consulting, reemphasized that transformation involves more than people, process, and technology. It also involves culture.

Anna Frazetto, the chief digital technology officer and president at Nash Tech Global, states that in her experience, company culture drives transformation and technological adoption in an organization.

"Think about it! It all starts with the top and the vision … The vision creates the culture. You hire with that in mind and before you know it, that is what shapes a company," she says. "I feel that the embedded culture is the bloodline of a company and it will drive success and must be understood before embarking on a transformation journey."

Culture is the critical factor in transformational efforts. It is both the prerequisite and the foundation for success. If you don't change the culture, the rest of your efforts will be wasted.

Without cultural transformation, the organization will continue following the same path it has followed for years or decades. "People will keep doing things the way they already know," Hendra says.

In the short term, you can force some modest behavioral changes through the introduction of new technologies, new processes, and new employees. You may win some battles—but you will lose the war.

That why we usually refer to transformation as a "strategy." It's not a series of steps—it's a holistic process with thousands of moving parts, unfolding over time and space.

For example, Hendra and her team recently helped a large multinational company stay on track over the course of its transformation, which included designing and building digital hubs in several countries. Additionally, the company needed to transform elements of its core technology stack, which required replacing systems, retraining managers, and hiring new groups of workers. The new technologies, processes, and people all had to fit together and operate smoothly within the company's culture, which was also adapting and evolving to keep pace with its customers. Fortunately, the company's CEO understood the complexity of the transformation and remained a steadfast champion through thick and thin. This sponsorship aspect of the equation is echoed by Frazetto:

> *Several times what I find is that the challenges are with the existing management team. The first step is getting buy-in and agreement from all the necessary participants. Once we establish that course of action, we break it down into smaller components ranging from the process to the staff and to the technology currently in place.*

The transformation referenced by Hendra has produced strong and consistently positive results in all of the company's markets, demonstrating the benefits of persevering in the face of monumental challenges.

Forging a Transformation Reality

When do business leaders first realize they need to do something different? Is there a definitive moment when a light bulb goes off, or is it a gradual process of realization?

The simple answer is, "All of the above." But in truth, most transformational strategies are born of fear. Companies talk and talk about transformation, but what finally gets them off the dime is having a competitor threatening to disrupt their core business model. That's when the talk turns into action.

Disruption comes in various sizes, shapes, and flavors. Different industries experience different kinds of disruption and must therefore develop different types of transformational strategies.

For example, companies operating in industries such as hospitality, retail, and financial services are generally more sensitive to quarterly results than companies in industries such as mining, manufacturing, and refining. That sensitivity usually influences the speed of their transformation. A company that worries about its quarterly earnings will probably transform itself faster than a company that doesn't.

Each industry has a moment when outside forces compel a major transformation. It's almost like a law of nature. In the retail banking industry, for instance, when one bank began offering mobile deposits, every other bank quickly followed suit. They really didn't have a choice—they had to transform or die.

The proliferation of smart personal devices has generated a continual race to innovate and win customers by offering conveniences and capabilities your competitors don't yet offer.

Companies in consumer-facing markets are racing to offer the best customer service, the best apps, and the best rewards programs. This is truly the new face of competition.

As Hendra observes, this continual race to outdo the competition means that every company must run at top speed just to stay in place. Innovating in this kind of environment requires nerves of steel and supernatural speed, neither of which are easily purchasable commodities.

So how do traditional companies remain competitive? Many respond to outside pressure by acquiring or merging with companies that specialize in rapid innovation. Sometimes they create entirely new companies that are spun off but remain in orbit around the parent company.

Recruiting, hiring, and retaining top talent is a major issue for companies to a far greater degree than ever before. Today, companies don't merely need talented people—they need super-talented people!

The talent conversation could not be a more pertinent one at this moment in time. Frazetto looks introspectively at the trajectory of change over just a few years: "I think life was simpler 10 years ago or even 5 years ago in comparison to today. So, when you marry technological advancements (harder skill required) with transformation and competitive pressures you wind up with the skill sets being compounded and getting more complex. No one ever looks for just one skill set any more."

Determined or Distraught?

Meredith Whalen is chief research officer at IDC and a member of the senior management team. She leads IDC's worldwide research organization, product management, marketing, and client services functions, setting the direction and agenda for IDC's worldwide research products. Her international team of 1,100 analysts leverage research and advisory services to empower business transformation for the Global 2000, and counsel technology suppliers on creating effective offerings for the digital economy.

I asked Meredith to help me understand why some organizations struggle with digital transformation, and she generously shared her team's research. According to their surveys, organizations with transformational goals fall into two categories: the "digitally determined" (46%) and the "digitally distraught" (54%) (see Figure 10.2).

"When we looked at the data, we saw common threads," Meredith explains. "The 'digitally determined' organizations make sure they're really executing on one strategy, one vision for digitally transforming the organization. They have an integrated enterprise-wide digital strategy."

By contrast, she notes, the "digitally distraught" organizations had multiple strategies. In some organizations, it seemed as though "each line of business or each functional area had its own digital transformation strategy and its own digital roadmap."

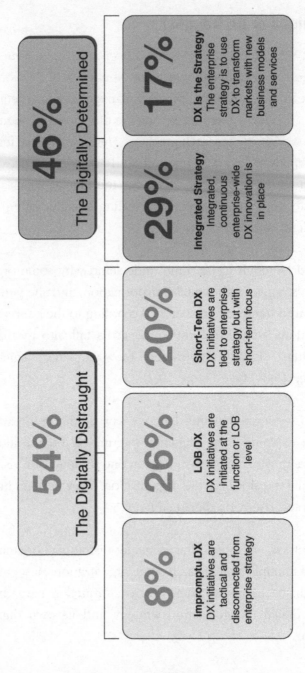

Figure 10.2 Source: IDC Global Leaders Survey North American sample, June 2018.

In a recent report, Meredith writes that becoming "digitally determined" requires more than grit and tenacity. It requires a blueprint with four essential components:

1. Create organizational alignment and culture around digital.

2. Employ a single enterprise-wide strategy.

3. Demonstrate inherent value of digital.

4. Scale digital innovations with an integrated platform.[1]

In our conversation, it became clear to me that leadership is a critical differentiator between "determined" and "distraught" organizations. "Transformation requires a top-down approach," Meredith says. "You need a CEO who says, 'I'm going to make the hard decisions and there will be changes here.' The 'digitally determined' are willing to do whatever it takes, even if it means upsetting the applecart."

Based on their findings, the IDC research team lists five key focus areas for "digitally determined" organizations:[2]

1. Creating digital KPIs

2. Establishing an end-state digital organizational structure

3. Constructing a long-term digital roadmap

---

[1] IDC PERSPECTIVE: A DX Blueprint from the Digitally Determined, by Meredith Whalen.

[2] IDC PERSPECTIVE: How to Break Through the Digital Transformation Deadlock, by Meredith Whalen.

4. Developing the most important digital capabilities

5. Building a digital platform

I found the IDC analysis to be especially useful, and I am grateful to Meredith for permitting me to quote from her reports and articles in this book. I also recommend reading Meredith's blog post, "The Digitally Determined Blueprint," in which she details the steps followed by successful organizations to achieve their transformational goals.[3]

Tone from the Top

Whether you end up with the much-desired streamlined ecosystem or poorly integrated islands of automation depends entirely on the tone from the top. A central strategy and appropriate funding for the right initiatives drives the planned and predetermined outcome, often exceeding expectations. A great strategy, but significant autonomy in downstream decision-making within organization P&L's can be disastrous in a digital transformation. The latter advances individual careers and generates impressive case studies of shiny new tech adoption but has a retarding effect on the overall transformation strategy.

More often than not, digital transformation is more impactful within well-run companies where there is a singular North Star and all decisions, investments, and attitudes follow that star.

---

[3] https://blogs.idc.com/2018/06/26/the-digitally-determined-blueprint/.

While not every aspect of these organizations works perfectly, they have developed a mindset and strategy that ensures alignment at almost all steps and back that up with a governance model that keeps the plan on its flight path. The outcomes are reflected in the results of organizations like these and the pace feels like a jet being catapulted off a carrier deck.

The obvious area where transformations typically fall flat is when business strategies are disconnected from execution plans, and while these disconnects become apparent early in the journey, the truly dangerous ones are when the strategy is subtly disconnected from the execution. Here is a brief list of issues that can derail a transformation project:

- Lack of process governance
- Minimal operational cadence
- Lack of formalized outcome tracking
- Vague predefined benefits identification
- Weak or non-dedicated project management
- Too many consultants and too few doers
- Lack of specific goals for key staff
- Poor technology decisions

Any of those issues has the potential to create redundant or unnecessary work for staff, resulting in missed deadlines and significant delays. Worse yet, endless rounds of "busy work" can yield the false impression that progress is imminent, despite the absence of measurable achievements.

Lack of staff motivation is an underlying and often critical issue that can engender low morale, lackluster performance, and a general sense of aimless confusion. Great leaders don't ignore the importance of motivation; they strive to maintain high levels of engagement, especially during periods of rapid change.

Net Takeaways

1. Transformation programs must be driven by a singular business strategy but can be broken down into multiple subprograms.

2. Transformation is a business strategy, not a series of technological advances.

3. Governance across the various activities along with technological investments must be centralized to allow for fewer integration challenges.

4. Progress reporting, project benefits measurement, and issue resolution must be tracked with regular and defined cadence.

5. Leverage design thinking for rapid problem solving where possible.

6. Seek informal feedback from casual conversations with employees, managers, and executives to get a feel for what's working and what could be improved.

7. Digital transformation is always defined in terms of business benefit.

Chapter 11

Use Case: The Smart City

Executive Summary: The impact of digital transformation extends far beyond the boundaries of corporations and business entities. Towns, cities, regions, and nations are also transforming themselves in the hope of providing better public services with greater efficiency, lower costs, less waste, and reduced carbon emissions.

Digital transformation is a truly global trend. Every region and demographic group is affected by the digitization of products and services. Within a brief span of time, we have become a digital world, driven by data and moving at the speed of information.

Today, our homes and communities are nodes in a worldwide digital network. The poet John Donne famously wrote that "no man is an island." Those words, published in 1624, seem eerily descriptive of our modern culture, in which we're never more than a tap away from connecting with friends on social media or reaching out to colleagues on a collaboration platform.

The impact of digital transformation extends far beyond the boundaries of corporations and business entities. One of the most compelling use cases for digital transformation is the smart city.

You've probably read about smart cities and wondered if they're real or just hype. I would say that smart cities are an emergent phenomenon, which makes them hard to describe. From my perspective, a smart city is a place where the continual collection and analysis of data enables the optimization of a broad portfolio of municipal services. A smart city provides the best possible experiences for its citizens, workers, and visitors—while simultaneously managing costs, improving efficiencies, and reducing energy consumption.

Although my description seems fairly straightforward, becoming a smart city can be complicated. Here's why: a city is a system of systems. Ideally, those systems should be interoperable and capable of sharing data. But the vast majority of cities were built long before the idea of systems thinking arose.

The systems we associate with a typical city—water, gas, electric, buses, subways, trash collection, sewage, streets, sidewalks, and parks—evolved separately, and often at different times, over the course of decades and centuries.

Most cities are disorganized tangles of disparate legacy systems. Data collection is haphazard and inconsistent. Some cities have made great strides in digitizing their data, yet many still keep records on paper and allow city departments to store their information in silos that are inaccessible to other departments.

The harsh truth is that most cities do not have a comprehensive data governance strategy. Cities without a clear data strategy will find it exceedingly difficult to use their data for analyzing and optimizing services on a consistent basis.

Smart cities, however, have strong data governance policies in place to ensure the accessibility of information across departments and agencies. Smart cities are all about good data management, and some smart cities have hired data scientists to oversee and facilitate the use of data in everyday decision-making processes.

For example, a smart city might use sensors and cameras to monitor activity in its parks. When nighttime activity in a park ebbs, the lights in the park could be dimmed to save energy. When people reenter the park, the lights would be brightened to full intensity. A smart city might also equip its senior citizens with a smart phone app that would automatically turn on the lights in a park when they enter, providing safer and more enjoyable experiences for people who might otherwise decide to stay at home.

A smart city would also keep track of activity patterns over time, enabling it to schedule maintenance and cleaning at times when the park is less crowded. Additionally, a smart city would monitor usage of its bike and walking trails to predict when repairs and maintenance will be necessary.

"A smart city will know when you're sick or injured and automatically dispatch emergency medics to help you," write Mike Barlow and Cornelia Lévy-Bencheton, co-authors of *Smart Cities, Smart Future*. "A smart city will remind you when it's time renew your driver's license—and then help you renew it from your mobile phone. A smart city will help you find a good rehabilitation center if your mom slips and falls on the sidewalk."

An Infinite Universe of Moving Parts

What can corporate executives learn from smart cities? I believe companies and cities encounter similar challenges when confronting the need for digital transformation. The first challenge is sheer complexity and the second challenge is managing risk. Here's a brief excerpt from *Smart Cities, Smart Future* describing the incredible complexity and inherent risk posed by cyber-physical systems in a metropolitan environment:

In a smart city, there are no standalone devices, applications or systems. Everything is connected and to some degree, interdependent.

For example, the ticket machines at the train station might seem like standalone devices, but they're connected to the city's transit, financial and electrical systems. Since the ticket machines accept credit cards in addition to cash, they're also connected to the privately owned and operated financial systems that process credit card payments.

Like the ticket machines, the small sensors in the subway that detect the approach of trains are both standalone devices and nodes in a network. Essentially, every device and application plays a dual role. It's an interesting phenomenon and a fundamental aspect of the Internet of Things (IoT).

Smart cities are subsets of the IoT, which means they are also subsets of the internet. That's more than a clever observation. It's a scary fact. The internet has many wonderful qualities, but security isn't one them.

As metaphorical children of the IoT and grandchildren of the internet, smart cities possess the strengths and weaknesses of their progenitors. They are broadly useful and usable. They are painfully difficult to secure. Security is to smart cities what kryptonite is to Superman.

Just as Superman's fear of kryptonite doesn't stop him from flying around and doing good deeds, smart cities must overcome their fear of cybercrime. We're not suggesting that cities should ignore the threat of cybercrime; we're saying that cities should acknowledge it and do everything in their power to fight it.[1]

---

[1] Barlow, M and Levy-Bencheton, C. (2018) *Smart Cities, Smart Future* (New York: Wiley).

Safety First

Because smart cities are cyber-physical systems, any digital transformation initiative must also take human safety and physical risks into account. In the corporate enterprise, we often use a risk assessment method called "C-I-A," which stands for confidentiality, integrity, and availability.

But smart cities are a blend of digital and physical assets. Real people, made of flesh and blood, live in smart cities, and we must consider the potential impact of our transformation project on their safety. For smart city transformation, the risk assessment method is "C-I-A + S," where the "S" stands for safety. Here's another brief excerpt from *Smart Cities, Smart Future*:

> *Safety throws a wrench into the traditional method of determining how much to spend protecting cyber assets. For years, the rule of thumb was simple: never spend more to protect an asset than the asset is worth.*
>
> *When safety is added to the equation, the rule of thumb goes out the window. For example, let's say the sensor in the subway car door costs three dollars. Does that mean you won't spend more than three dollars protecting it, even when you know that if it fails, a rider might be hurt?*
>
> *If a subway car door closes on a rider's hand or foot, the cost of the injury will far exceed the cost of the sensor in the door. If the injured rider decides to sue the city, the cost will be even higher.*

Smart cities will have to invent new ways of modeling risk, valuing assets and setting spending priorities. If the emergency braking system in a smart elevator is hacked and the elevator plunges 100 floors before hitting the ground, the first thought in everyone's mind won't be the cost of the elevator.

Six Areas of "Smartness"

In their book, Barlow and Lévy-Bencheton list six focus areas that broadly define the smart city concept:

1. **Smart Economy.** Multiple economic components from the public and private sectors are integrated, coordinated, and orchestrated to speed the flow of resources and materials to projects and areas of the city where they are most needed.

2. **Smart Government.** Decisions are made and resources are allocated based on actual needs of citizens and predicted usage of services, as opposed to guesswork, BAU (business as usual), or fleeting political sentiment.

3. **Smart Environment.** Smart cities use data analytics to trim energy costs and reduce carbon emissions. They also follow "circular economy" principles to ensure the lowest achievable levels of consumption and waste.

4. **Smart Living.** Services and resources are optimized to ensure widest possible accessibility, usage, and enjoyment across all demographic groups and sections of the city. In other words, the benefits of city living are shared

broadly, rather than being limited to small groups of privileged users.

5. **Smart People.** Education, lifelong learning, and continual re-skilling are prioritized and fully funded, fostering and promoting a culture of intellectual curiosity, innovation, and invention.

6. **Smart Mobility.** Smart cities have fully integrated multimodal transit and transportation systems, ensuring easy travel and commuting across all sections of the city and its surrounding suburbs.

Achieving success in each of the six focus areas depends on strong marriages of policy and technology. You can no longer have one without the other; they have become the yin and yang of modern civilization.

"The smart city movement is part of a larger digital revolution," the authors write. "Digital technologies aren't simply transforming business and industry—they're transforming each and every aspect of our lives, including the places where we live. We are experiencing a genuine shift of paradigms; a new world is being born."

Four Stages of Evolution

Another important lesson we can learn from smart cities is the importance of moving forward in a series of steps. I'm not huge fan of incremental change, but I do appreciate the value of putting one foot in front of the other. There's nothing wrong with treading carefully, especially when large amounts of money are at stake.

Many smart cities learned this lesson the hard way, buying into the notion that technology was the answer to all of their problems. Some of the early adopters realized the error of their ways, scaling back their efforts and redefining their objectives. Over time, it became apparent that smart cities aren't built in a day. Even the "smartest" cities follow an evolutionary path with four stages:

1. **Tech-driven.** Cities rely on vendors and consultants to guide choices and invest in technology solutions.

2. **City led.** Local government takes the reins and develops its own strategies for smart city development.

3. **Citizen-centric.** Citizens become more involved in the process, developing grassroots programs for positive change and pushing back against top-down initiatives.

4. **Collaborative.** In this stage, coalitions of engaged stakeholders work collaboratively to develop practical and sustainable smart city strategies aimed at solving real-world challenges such as transportation, public safety, accessibility, inclusion, and economic opportunity.

"Sooner or later, most of us will live in smart cities," the authors write. "It's up to us to determine whether those cities are smart because they're equipped with the latest technology solutions or smart because they provide us with the resources we need to live happy and fulfilling lives."

The insights drawn by the authors of *Smart Cities, Smart Future* can be generalized to cover virtually all forms of digital transformation strategy. The primary lesson is that a successful transformation project always focuses on people first and technology last. It's never just about technology; it's about people using technology to make their lives easier, happier, and more satisfying.

Net Takeaways

1. Leaders of corporate transformation strategies can learn valuable lessons from smart cities, which face similar challenges and problems.

2. Smart cities remind us that all successful transformation efforts depend primarily on changing the habits and behaviors of people. The technology is secondary.

3. Complexity is part of the challenge, for the smart city and the modern enterprise. Ignoring or downplaying the complexity of a transformation project will guarantee poor results.

Chapter 12

Looking Ahead: Runway or Precipice?

Executive Summary: Many of the new terms bandied about today are essentially buzzwords. But not everything you see or hear is hype. There are serious challenges ahead, and you must prepare your organization and yourself for handling them effectively. This chapter is basically a list of newer technologies, with advice and suggestions for avoiding missteps.

A Google search for the term "digital transformation" will yield nearly half a million results in less than a second. A search for "artificial intelligence" will generate even more results in about the same fraction of a second. Searching for terms such as "machine learning," "virtual reality," "big data," "robotics," "predictive analytics," "blockchain," and "quantum computing" will yield generally similar results.

If you work in the field of business or technology, you can be certain that people will be asking you for your opinion on the above mentioned terms. My advice is to be prepared. Have simple, easy answers ready—because the questions will be asked, I guarantee you!

With that thought in mind, here are some of the responses I typically give when asked about the latest, greatest developments in tech.

Artificial Intelligence

AI still induces a combination of fear and skepticism in most people. From my perspective as a business executive, only a handful of AI solutions are mature enough to be readily adopted. In other words, AI is highly promising, but it's not ready for prime time.

In summary, AI has a lot of promise and is progressing steadily but before trying to leverage it within a business the basic rules still apply—garbage in/garbage out.

If posed with an investment decision, focus the conversation around the quality of data that will drive intelligent outcomes, not necessarily just the volume. Good business process will lead to better opportunities to leverage artificial intelligence.

Blockchain

Blockchain is definitely not for everyone. Much has been made about this technology because it is the foundational technology of modern cryptocurrencies. Blockchain itself is not cryptocurrency, but it supports cryptocurrency transactions.

But in layman's terms let's boil it down to a simpler context. Imagine that we have a small company with offices in New York, London, and Singapore, all working off a single expense record book. Here's the "traditional" scenario:

- The New York office keeps the record book and the other two offices update the book when they incur an expense.

- Only the New York office is aware of all transactions across the three offices.

- In the event of a security breach in any of the three locations, information could be altered for fraudulent purposes with relatively little chance of detection.

In a "blockchain" scenario, each office is a "node" in a secure network and each of the offices would have access to the most current version of the record book in real time. If, for example, the London office incurred an expense, the record would be validated with the other two offices and the encrypted blockchain would be updated.

A security breach at one office would not compromise the network; attackers would have to breach all three nodes to succeed. Attempting to breach all three nodes would require a tremendous amount of computing power, which is why blockchain is considered more secure than traditional methods of keeping records.

So far, blockchain has proven useful for validating complex supply chains, moving valuable cargo, cryptocurrency, money transfers, land titles, copyrights, and so on with an ever-increasing list. Being in early stages of adoption, there are very few examples of its full-blown use. It will be some time before there is enough maturity in the market where use cases become more frequent.

If posed with an investment decision, be aware that blockchain exchanges are starting to become a service provided by the big cloud providers due to their heavy computing requirements. Just like cloud providers that slowly proliferated the technology market, Blockchain-as-a-Service (BaaS) will provide more opportunities for organizations to leverage this technology.

Robotics

Robots have learned to ride bicycles, assemble cars, defuse bombs, and deliver groceries. But don't hold your breath waiting for them to take over your office job.

From a business perspective, robots (aka "bots") mostly handle process automation tasks. Bots can do the mundane, repetitive, and voluminous tasks that people really don't enjoy doing. This kind of robotics is called robotics process automation (RPA), and is rapidly becoming one of the common types of automation. It works best when the organization already has orderly, well-established, and tightly governed processes.

RPA was traditionally called scripting and has been around from the early days of software coding; when developers would write software modules that did repetitive tasks, these modules would then be "summoned" within the context of a larger computing transaction. The simple difference between traditional scripting and modern robotics is that software companies have made it into platforms that are abstracted from software code and can be written by using relatively natural language terminology.

Scripts or bots can be written and integrated to almost any platform out there. For example, if you run Oracle, Microsoft, or SAP as a financial accounting software, RPA platforms from companies such as UI Path and Automation Anywhere can run process automation independent of that accounting software. They automate processes to mimic what a typical user would do repetitively.

Case studies show that RPA as a technology is very useful but many organizations are not culturally ready for it and some level of digital proficiency would help remove the employee fear factor and leverage the technology for what it is. The large management consulting organizations, financial firms, and life insurance are a few industries that use robotics extensively, effectively, and glean great benefits from it. I have seen other industries use RPA to prepare large data sets for analytics, speed up back-office processes, and help get products quicker to market. Robotics, though often associated with taking over repetitive human tasks, poses a higher risk for business process outsourcers (BPOs). Many companies already have their back and middle office work outsourced and leverage some form of labor arbitrage that very outsourced labor will steadily be automated and will force the renegotiation of contracts. Some companies are taking a proactive stance and offering better pricing as a result of internal automation.

If faced with an internal investment decision, ask questions around the business problem it will solve first. Then ask questions around quality and governance of the business processes. Needless to say, it's easier to understand process automation when the process is streamlined and much harder when the process is fragmented. RPA done right can deliver solutions to complex business challenges and yield efficiency and cost savings while doing so.

Virtual Reality

It was the peak of winter and I was piloting a Boeing 777 aircraft into John F. Kennedy airport in New York with over 280 passengers on board. I turned on the seatbelt signs as strong winds buffeted my aircraft and I lined up for runway 4L. That's when the rain and hail started. Visibility was low and I was relying purely on my cockpit instruments; I wasn't sure I'd be able to land when the tower cleared me on my final approach. The landing was too fast and way too hard. I bounced twice, sped down the runway, brakes screeching, engines in reverse and I still skidded off the end of the runway to come to a complete stop. Then I sat back in relief and took a sip of my coffee while not caring what happened to my passengers.

The coffee was real, the aircraft wasn't.

It was the nearest bad-weather "reality" scenario I could muster with the limited knowledge of my favorite hobby, flight simulation. In virtual reality mode it feels like the real thing!

In another similar scenario, the movie *Avatar* in 3D was awe-inspiring for me as the immersive scenes caused one to move through large objects that defied gravity while dragons flew around.

There is a subtle difference between the two scenarios; while a 3D movie places you in the magic of the moment, you just watch and react to thrilling events in the film that can be entirely imaginary. Virtual reality on the other hand creates visual or interactive spaces with a computer-generated three-dimensional environment based on real-life scenarios, like an aircraft landing while sitting in the pilot's seat.

In order to do this, one needs a couple of simple pieces of technology equipment, usually a headset and a controller—the headset to view the images or specific objects within the 3D environment, think of it as a mouse pointer, and the controller to take action. For example, if driving in a virtual car, the controller can be a steering wheel and pedals, or for a virtual flight, a flight yoke, and so on. Whatever the application, you are removed from the world around you in a completely immersive experience.

People often confuse virtual reality with "augmented reality." The latter actually enables apps on devices to insert objects into live scenarios. The best example of this was the Pokémon craze a few years ago. By pointing your phone camera at certain areas, for example, street intersections, parks, or other such locations, you could see the presence of a Pokémon character at the location—they were augmenting the reality of your surroundings while you were present at the location.

Virtual reality has been around for a while but newer technology and commercialization of headsets and controllers has made it more accessible to consumers.

The premise is that VR is so immersive that we will be able to recreate any physical world task or interaction within the virtual space and train our employees, give customers the closest experience of really driving the car they want to buy, show customers what the first-class cabin experience really looks like, stand at the edge of Niagara Falls, or walk through Machu Picchu. For the first time gamification of customer experience and training scenarios do really sound like fun.

Could there be applications for patients who are bedridden to get a few moments of escape or physical therapy landscapes better than the sterile environments of a doctor's office? I could cite at least 15 different application opportunities to use VR but the ideas are only as limited as your thinking will allow.

If faced with an internal technology investment question, consider your type of business: Is it customer experience-based or would it be better utilized for internal training purposes? Almost all industries have the potential to benefit from the virtual reality ecosystem—from content creators to experience creators such as digital marketing units to business and retail consumers. While costs could vary depending on the scale of the undertaking, a well-designed memorable experience is priceless and puts you on the cutting edge of modern tech.

Big Data

How big is BIG? I was involved in a project where our data group was in an experimental stage with a database technology company, a Silicon Valley startup. In order to test their capability, the group decided to send them a small file. When I queried what "small" meant, I found that the database had 65 million records!

When large trucks pulled up outside our offices to collect boxes of permanent financial records, we never called it "big paperwork." In fact, the old paper-based management of transactions, be they financial, retail, or business related, had extremely limited value for mining or analyzing the data within. In the environment we live in today, almost every transaction from sensors in vehicles, factory machinery, online retail databases, search engines, points in a supply chain, Internet browsers, game consoles, smart TVs, cell phone towers, smart watches, voice activated devices, or your car GPS all generate data outputs from a transaction or data touchpoints from interacting with other devices or people. These volumes of data are undoubtedly large and can yield valuable information if mined or analyzed. Given these volumes, technologies are now available to segment, dissect, and analyze meaningful patterns and outputs to support business decisions, wear and tear on equipment, utilization of machinery, and many, many more uses.

This data due to its voluminous and seemingly ever-growing scale is often referred to as "big data." The advantages are plenty and even small businesses are able to benefit from this method of capturing and analyzing outcomes from data as they take advantage of affordable and easily accessible cloud-based technology services.

If faced with an investment decision, discuss the benefits of personalization, decision support, field maintenance, and customer service by using the analyzed data to your business advantage. And while benefits may vary, issues related to data privacy must be clearly addressed with any scenario. Some organizations using this data capability may have a relatively small geographical footprint but even though big data tends to be anonymized, a good thumb rule is to take the most stringent global privacy rules and apply them to your environment. This can be a confusing and complicated area and if a "data privacy officer" is not a designated role in your organization, professional legal advice should be sought.

Cloud

"Islands of automation" was a term coined in the early days of network computing to indicate limitations of interconnectivity between computer systems. Companies often maintained local computing centers in each of their locations, called data centers. Later in the evolution of networking, wide area networks (WANs) started creating better interconnected systems with less duplication of servers and applications. With the proliferation of network connectivity, centralization of these data centers was the next stage of consolidation but these centers were still extremely expensive to run; they had to have back-up data centers for disaster recovery; they had to maintain efficient cooling systems to handle the heat generated by the computer equipment; often they occupied expensive real estate; and they had to be monitored 24 hours a day, 7 days a week, 365 days a year. But most importantly, they were never fully utilized. For the most part, systems ran at peak during business hours and sat idle in off hours; even round-the-clock operations could not efficiently utilize all the available computing power of servers.

Over time, this morphed into a solution where the hardware and network was built up by service providers and made available to buyers in bite-sized chunks—this came to be known as cloud computing. By way of a simple analogy, cloud computing is similar to a hotel. You go in and rent some space with all the amenities of heating, cooling, plumbing, secure access, etc. You can upgrade if you wish, or take the bargain rate, and you can also buy more space and stay for longer or checkout when you're done, but you would never have to build or buy your own hotel. Cloud computing works on a similar concept. You buy the computing power, network, and storage for the capacity you need for a fully functioning data center.

This capability has widened to a broader ecosystem of "managed services" or cloud-based applications where the vendor or supplier provides an end-to-end method of a given service, for example, Gmail or Office365, where all you need is a contract and a browser to make it work. This does not imply that you don't need some of those technology skills internally; in almost all cases integration to other systems, including security and access to these systems, is handled internally.

If faced with an investment decision, it is crucial to get your internal technology architects involved early. Cloud contracts related to data retention and transfer can also be complex. While most cloud vendors have figured out the best ways to resolve this, "vendor lock-in" can be a serious problem if you decide to change providers in the next few years. Also question where your data resides; if in another country, what laws apply. What failover options they have for disaster recovery and understanding their integration capabilities for today, as well as a roadmap of the future, are crucial. There is also the concept of private cloud, public cloud, and hybrid cloud—but leave that to your architects to decide the right approach for your business.

Internet of Things

You've probably received notification emails for when your credit card payment is due or your online order has shipped. But that casual method of notification is relatively passé compared to the sensor in your car telling you the inflation level in your tires in real time, or your dishwasher telling your maintenance company of a potential issue, or the motion sensor in your thermostat adjusting the room temperature based on activity in that area.

Sensors are now being built into everything and are connected to deliver their bits of information to other sensors that trigger a reaction or send information to relevant recipients to take action very rapidly, not like the old methods of asynchronous email.

Industrial use of sensors have been around for a while; over a decade ago a large microchip manufacturer was able to tell the age of fresh produce being transported by attaching a small RFID chip to the inside of a shipping container. Wearable technologies help workers build planes while reducing exhaustion from carrying heavy equipment. Sensors in tractors in fields thousands of miles away can inform a monitoring center of a breakdown or even help prevent one.

However, in today's scenario, sensors are now placed into everything we touch and create ecosystems that presumably support our every human convenience. If you want to check your heart rate while at the gym, just glance at your watch. If you want to see who rang your doorbell while you're in another city, just glance at your phone. You can even open doors remotely for your kids by hitting that smartlock app—and the list goes on.

This is the hyperconnected world we live in and refer to as the "Internet of Things" (IoT). IoT is here to stay and enables a world where these connected sensors provide invaluable conveniences and save time and money for a generation glued to interactive handheld devices. Many industries have capitalized on this and continue to invest in IoT in innovative ways as seen here.

If faced with an investment decision, the technology is constantly evolving and there are companies that can assist with every aspect of your business needs if you choose to go with IoT. The important questions would be more around user experience (also known as UX), what data will you collect, what information would you glean from data sensors in your product, and how you will respond to that information. Will you improve service, will it be used to improve the product itself, will you use it to cross-sell, would the data help drive acquisition strategy to fill strategic needs gaps? The opportunities are tremendous.

Marketing Automation and Programmatic Advertising

You search online for an airline ticket and you coincidentally start receiving emails with destination guides, discount tours, airline perks and benefits, maybe even a credit card tied to specific airlines. Congratulations, you are most likely the successful target of a marketing automation program. This is not bad news as you will get information relevant to that initial search and it also means that marketers have data on your persona and can connect with you through multiple channels.

Typically within the business landscape that persona is managed by a customer relationship management (CRM) platform where various pieces of information about a customer are stored, including last contact, nature of contact, and potential for a sale or contract, etc. This in turn allows for targeted marketing campaigns with focused information. The process of being able to serve up an offer to a buyer in an automated way through multiple digital touchpoints is often referred to as marketing automation.

But what happens when great CRM platforms are not available?

One nuance of marketing automation in the digital space is called programmatic advertising. A simple form of how this works is outlined below. For example:

- A user browses the Internet; data management platforms (DMPs) constantly collect and analyze cookies off the user's browser. This analysis creates a target audience profile and a better view of the customer's online profile through search, and so on.

- In order to make good use of these profiles and post them on various online properties, the intermediary between the data platform and the supplier is the demand-side platform (DSP). This platform evaluates the impression based on certain data points and submits a bid to the supplier.

- Publishers manage their online inventory on supplier-side platforms that keep track of the unsold inventory; they also pick from the highest bidder for available inventory.

- The end result of the above three steps is that an ad is served to a user online.

There are different reasons for bids to be higher or lower, as an example:

- One of them may be brand awareness, and position on a webpage may not be as important as long as it appears frequently on as many web pages as possible.

- Another reason may be that the brand wants a distinct call to action and wants the user to click for more information or to buy a product. These would be placed strategically on the webpage and are often referred to as "above the fold," as in a folded newspaper, where you see the headline first.

Programmatic advertising is advancing as a result of the technologies mentioned above, such as AI, big data, and robotics, and has increasingly matured for television as well as connected TVs, to become part of the Internet ecosystem. Opportunities to assign ads based on television content or target audience increase as the inclination of consumers to use video on demand and other streaming methods, also referred to as "nonlinear TV," increases. The method by which you cannot pause or forward ads is referred to as "linear TV."

If faced with an investment decision, consider engaging specialized digital agencies to run this for you, especially if you are a small to medium-sized business.

Large companies often make the investment in the overall platform and engage digital agencies to support parts of it due to its various specializations. This is an involved, always-on type of ecosystem and needs skills that can handle managing branding, brand awareness, customer engagement, and customer conversion through e-commerce platforms.

Even though attribution for the quote "Data is the new oil" is not clear, it has some relevance here. If you've worked with oil, you know it's messy and needs to go through a process before it is usable in an internal combustion engine.

Similarly, marketing automation also has a significant data play and analysts and data scientists work behind the scenes to cleanse data and manage these complex platforms before the data is in a usable format, which makes internalizing and supporting this platform a serious consideration.

Don't Get Fooled Again...

Have you ever seen an ad for a great product in a glossy magazine, only to order it and receive a piece of cheap molded plastic? It happens less often with the onset of Internet reviews, but it does happen.

Applications work pretty much the same way. While most modern applications have all the makings of a solid foundation, some applications just have glossy exteriors. These apps are easy to create with tools readily available to a 12-year-old with an interest in building them. However, we see more often than not that senior executives succumb to the "look and feel" of an application or platform rather than its underlying framework.

Think of a sleek Formula One car body with a motorcycle engine. Similarly, application architecture can be complex and should not be decided on based on just its look and feel.

From the early 1980s, the Open Systems Interconnection (OSI) model has helped create a logical breakdown for interconnected networks and application protocols. While a lot of the methods are used to create apps, the fundamental way they interact with the network remains the same. Even within a cloud environment the basic logic of the OSI model is still applicable.

The OSI model contains seven layers and is a good teaching tool, as annotated below:

7. Application

6. Presentation

5. Session

4. Transport

3. Network

2. Data

1. Physical

This is not meant to be a technical explanation of each layer but I've often used this analogy with executives to show them just one dimension of the complexity that sits under the glossy exterior of the application or Layer 7 that they might be looking at. Applications have their own sets of integration options with terms like *application programing interfaces* (APIs), *service-oriented architectures* (SOAs) and other gnarly expressions only suitable for use by integration gurus.

If faced with an investment decision, bring in your technology architects early—then trust their evaluation. No matter how great an app looks, if your architect says it is a risky proposition, it most likely is.

Newer technological advancements are more complex than ever before. New terminology and acronyms already proliferate our conversations and it's hard to keep up with an understanding of each and every one of them.

Digital transformation leaders need to be skilled in the art of storytelling. They have to break down these complex technological advancements into relatable experiences for their audiences in the boardroom and the back office. Furthermore, they have to leverage their digital proficiency skills in order to make the right transformative decisions while maintaining an innovative edge at all times.

Net Takeaways

1. New technologies and their acronyms will come and go; always focus your investment decision on the core business purpose.

2. Involve professionals to objectively evaluate the underpinnings of modern data services or technology offerings that you want to acquire.

3. Familiarize yourself with the fundamental aspects of the new technology and explain them to your audiences with practical analogies.

Chapter 13

AI: The Elephant in the Room

Mike Barlow[1]

Whether you are a C-suite executive, line of business (LOB) manager, or a learning and development (L&D) strategist in the human resources department, you are probably dealing with questions and concerns about the looming impact of artificial intelligence (AI) on the workplace.

---

[1] Mike Barlow is an award-winning journalist, prolific author, and business strategy consultant. He is the author of *Learning to Love Data Science* and coauthor of *Smart Cities, Smart Future*. He is also the author of many articles, reports, and papers on topics such as artificial intelligence, machine learning, digital transformation, and IT architecture.

For senior executives, AI will raise difficult questions about:

- Remaining relevant in rapidly evolving markets.
- Competing effectively against faster-moving opponents.
- Existential risks and long-term business strategies.

For LOB managers, AI will raise concerns about:

- Keeping pace with new technologies.
- Reskilling and upskilling employees.
- Adapting to change, both internally and externally.

For L&D leaders, concerns will include:

- Meeting the needs of business units.
- Developing skills and talent within the organization.
- Evaluating quality and content of learning tools and solutions.

If you are uncertain and unsure about AI, don't worry—you're in good company. Some of the world's most experienced data scientists say it's difficult to separate truth from fantasy in conversations about AI.

"There's always been a lot of hype surrounding AI. One of the early definitions was 'AI is all the stuff that doesn't work yet,' and there's a fair bit of truth in that," says Ted Dunning, a seminal figure in the data science community and early pioneer of big data applications.

AI covers a broad swath of territory from machine learning (ML) to neural networks to logistic regression. *Natural language processing* (NLP) and *robotic process automation* (RPA) are commonly tossed into discussions about AI, along with terms like *deep learning* (DL), *reinforcement learning* (RL), and *convolutional networks*.

"People use grandiose terms when they talk about AI, but what's important to remember is that we're trying to solve serious problems and do something useful," says Dunning, who serves as chief application architect for MapR, a data platform for AI and analytics. "I don't care whether the solution looks intelligent or not. If it solves a complex problem we couldn't solve before, that's all that really matters."

What Artificial Intelligence Is and Isn't

"Think of AI as an airplane," says Lynda Chin, a medical doctor and former department chair and professor of genomic medicine at the University of Texas MD Anderson Cancer Center, as well as scientific director of the MD Anderson Institute for Applied Cancer Science. "An airplane will get you from Point A to Point B, but you have to know where you are going and how to fly an airplane."

Like flying an airplane, using AI effectively requires prodigious amounts of training and practice. "When a new surgical tool is invented, surgeons cannot simply begin using it on patients," says Dr. Chin. "They need to train and practice first. It's the same with AI."

Modern technologies such as airplanes and advanced surgical devices have changed our lives dramatically. Yet they haven't eliminated the basic needs they were created to address. People still need to travel and when they get sick or injured, they want to get better.

AI is a relatively new invention. It is not, however, a philosopher's stone that will magically turn lead into gold. Like most inventions of the human mind, AI will make our lives more convenient, but not necessarily easier or less complicated.

"AI is a very powerful tool that can help human beings in routine physical and intellectual tasks," says Vijay Tallapragada of the National Oceanic and Atmospheric Administration (NOAA), which provides weather forecasts, storm warnings, navigational information, and scientific data to public, private, and academic organizations.

Tallapragada heads the Modeling and Data Assimilation Branch at NOAA's Environmental Modeling Center in College Park, Maryland. He's also acting chief of NOAA's Coupling and Dynamics Group. As a practicing data scientist, he watches developments in AI very closely.

"With AI, you can quickly scan a large database of images or records, rapidly classify multiple objects of various kinds, and uncover hidden relationships in vast amounts of data," he says. "But it's not a universal key that can open any door."

AI at a Glance

What it can do ...	What it cannot do ...
Scan quickly through big data and find records or images that meet prespecified conditions	Smoothly manage challenges posed by "large problem spaces" such as autonomous driving and complex robotic manufacturing scenarios
Reveal hidden patterns and subtle relationships in large quantities of data	Replace high-skill workers, team leaders, and executives
Provide scientists and marketers with fresh insights and ideas	Think for itself

Adaptive Business Process Transformation

From an organizational perspective, AI is ushering in a new wave of business transformation. In *Human + Machine: Reimagining Work in the Age of AI*, coauthors Paul R. Daugherty and H. James Wilson list three waves of transformation:

1. **Standardized.** Assembly lines for mass manufacturing of products for global markets.

2. **Automated.** Business process reengineering and digitalization to create new business models and new industries.

3. **Adaptive.** Innovative, ongoing partnerships between human and machine intelligence to create continually evolving products and services for digitally connected markets.

We're entering the third wave now, in which the relationships between people and machines will evolve continuously for decades. In other words, the nature of work will evolve to match the pace of technology development.

"The third wave has created a huge, dynamic, and diverse space in which humans and machines collaborate to attain orders-of-magnitude increases in business performance," write Daugherty and Wilson.

For many, the idea of keeping up with artificial intelligence and other advanced technologies will seem frightening. But the greater risk is ignoring them or misunderstanding their potential value. Like it or not, we are developing symbiotic relationships with our machines. The quality of those relationships will depend heavily on our ability to understand the potential—and the limitations—of machine intelligence.

Debunking Myths About Artificial Intelligence

Even before the term *artificial intelligence* was coined by computer scientist John McCarthy in 1956, people have been fascinated by the idea of "thinking machines" and "electronic brains." Smart robots, whether good or evil, have become stock characters in science fiction; AI itself has become a virtually inexhaustible source of legend and lore.

The dense thicket of mythology that has sprung up around AI is not particularly helpful to practitioners in the real world, says Josh Patterson, an experienced data scientist who consults on big data applications and applied machine learning. AI is neither alive nor self-aware, Patterson says.

"AI today in real terms is applied machine learning," he says. "Folks who over-market machine learning to be 'general artificial intelligence' do the entire computer science industry a disservice. Machine learning is classification and regression, and in no way matches up to ephemeral aspirations of an all-knowing, self-aware system."

If AI isn't what everyone seems to think it is, then why all the hoopla? What set the stage for the sudden popularity of AI?

"What changed was the exponential increase in computing power, coupled with a fall in costs, and the mass proliferation of data in recent years. This enabled data science to alter the paradigm of AI research, supplanting a field that was once logic-based with one that simulates *learning* through statistical models—we call this machine learning," explains Daryl Kang, a data scientist at Forbes and a graduate of Columbia University's Data Science Institute.

Machine learning, which essentially enables software to "learn" from data, is not a novel technique. "I do not make as strong a distinction between AI and machine learning as some people do," says Ellen Friedman, principal technologist at MapR. "I see AI as a trendier term and maybe a subset of machine learning."

Both terms and the processes they represent, she notes, "have been around for a *long* time—some of the hype, especially around AI, is new, but artificial intelligence and machine learning are not new."

Still, a lot has changed recently, she adds, including:

- Much larger scale and wider variety of data to inform machine-made decisions;

- Better and more practical technology and architectures to deliver the data and models;

- Better algorithms and, in some cases, pre-built models that can be customized, leading to dramatically better results on some classically difficult problems such as vision or speech recognition and translations;

- A *much* broader recognition of the value and feasibility of AI and machine learning; and

- As a consequence of these changes, AI has been democratized and is more widely used than ever before.

For LOB managers, the rise of AI ramps up expectations and fuels dreams of continuous improvement in almost every area. Don't be surprised when the C-suite peppers you with questions about how your teams are deploying AI and advanced analytics to create competitive advantages and efficiencies for the company.

Remember, AI is no longer considered pie in the sky. It's not "over the horizon" or "around the next bend in the road." AI has left the laboratory and is already proving its value in areas such as healthcare, education, transportation, public safety, retailing, marketing, telecommunications, entertainment, manufacturing, construction, energy, pharmaceuticals, supply chain management, and predictive maintenance. All of us have a stake in making sure that our organizations make the most of it.

Finding Needles in Haystacks

AI's ability to find unseen patterns in huge mountains of data makes it especially valuable to scientific researchers and commercial marketers. For researchers, AI promises to deliver a new generation of tailor-made drugs and medical therapies. For marketers, AI offers a bottomless treasure chest of golden opportunities for selling, cross-selling, and upselling.

Applying AI to retail transaction data sets, for example, can reveal precisely which combinations of products shoppers buy when they go to a supermarket or home furnishings store. AI-generated insights enable retailers to stock products when and where shoppers are most likely to buy them.

AI also allows retailers to offer discounts and schedule special sales events without having to guess about the buying habits of their customers.

AI has the potential to transform many aspects of our lives. But it still takes human judgment to recognize the value of the insights AI can reveal. In other words, AI can find patterns in data that are invisible to human eyes, but not every pattern discovered by AI is inherently valuable. An AI itself has no clue whether the patterns it discovers are important or relevant. To an AI, all patterns are purely mathematical.

"Maybe the simplest view of AI is that it is machine-assisted decision making," says Friedman. "AI is not magic. It requires good-quality and appropriate data, an understanding of that data, a well-formed question or basis for analysis, the right algorithm or algorithms, a ton of efficient logistics for data and model management, and a way to take practical action on the output of the AI process."

Areas of rapid AI growth and adoption

- Healthcare
- Education
- Transportation
- Public Safety
- Retailing
- Manufacturing

- Marketing

- Entertainment

- Energy

- Pharmaceuticals

- Telecommunications

- Supply Chain Management and Logistics

- Predictive Maintenance

Will AI Replace Your Employees?

The rise of AI has also led to fears of massive unemployment and economic dislocation. Undoubtedly, AI will have a major impact on the job market. Some areas of work will be affected more quickly than others.

At call centers and help desks, the changes will be drastic. Many jobs will disappear and the remaining jobs will be transformed. Accountants, paralegals, cashiers, and welders may largely vanish from the workforce. The changes will also affect people with advanced degrees and certificates, such as radiologists, insurance brokers, and financial planners.

The bottom line is that AI will take over thousands of routine or repetitive tasks now performed by humans. If your job *can* be automated, it *will* be automated. Wholesale automation of customer service operations will likely wreak economic havoc in countries such as India, the Philippines, and Poland, which have invested heavily in call centers.

Automation will affect people at every strata of the workforce. For the moment, robotic process automation (RPA) focuses mainly on highly repetitive tasks. But when AI is fully baked into process automation, all knowledge workers will feel the pain.

The good news is that shiny metal robots with glowing red eyes won't be taking our jobs. The bad news is that AI chatbots, which seem cute and harmless, are likely to eliminate or displace many roles in the modern workplace.

For example, it seems unlikely that the role of administrative assistant will survive the next wave of chatbot development. "Soon we'll be saying, 'Tell your bot to call my bot,' when we need to schedule a meeting or set up a video conference," says a leading technology executive.

New areas of bot specialization are already emerging within the field of data science. In an excellent column on the impact of AI on labor markets in the U.S. and India, Pulitzer Prize–winning columnist Thomas Friedman writes of new jobs such as "digital conversation designers" and "voice conversation designers."[2]

For data scientists specializing in AI chatbot design, the goal is creating bots that can accurately gauge a customer's intent before handing the interaction off to a human. Chatbot

---

[2]"A.I. Still Needs H.I. (Human Intelligence), for Now," by Thomas Friedman, Opinion, *The New York Times*, Feb. 26, 2019.

designers measure the amount of time it takes before a human agent must intervene and create a score that serves as their "AI batting average," Friedman writes.

From a cost-benefit perspective, it makes sense to automate roles that don't require years of experience. But eliminating those roles can send dangerous ripples through organizations and cultures, since many people begin their careers in entry-level jobs. AI-powered automation might be a logical choice for many organizations, but there will be legions of unintended and unforeseen consequences for future generations of workers.

Is There a Difference Between AI and Data Science?

Which came first, data science or AI? Unlike the chicken–egg conundrum, this one's easy to answer. Data science has been around in one form or another for centuries, while AI dates back to the 1950s. Data science is foundational to AI; without data science, there would be no AI.

But there are critical differences. "Data science is the study of extracting value from data while AI is the ability of machines to perceive and to adapt to changes in their environment through actions that optimize their objectives," Kang says.

Here's a rough visualization: imagine a pyramid with statistics at the base, data science in the middle, and AI at the top.

If you want to get fancy, add a layer of machine learning in between data science and AI.

"Data science guides everything that sets up the machine learning," says Sandy Silk, director of IT Security Education and Consulting at Harvard University. "We need the data scientists to figure out the appropriate algorithms and data models to use, validate that the underlying data sets are large enough and diverse enough to accurately reflect the population they're intended to serve, and to verify that the produced results are accurate and not biased."

For example, let's say you apply for a home mortgage loan from a bank. If the bank's machine-learning model recommends against approving your application, it should be required to explain why. "There needs to be clarity about the data elements that led to the result," Silk says. "The model can't be a black box of mystery."

In *Weapons of Math Destruction*, mathematician Cathy O'Neil tells the story of a school district that hired a data science company to analyze the performance of teachers. Based on the company's analysis, the district fired some of its best teachers. How did that happen?

It turned out the company's algorithms weren't up to the task of evaluating teachers in real-life classrooms. But when the fired teachers protested, the district sided with the algorithms.

Algorithms are basically sequences of instructions for computers to follow. As O'Neil points out, you cannot appeal to an algorithm. "They do not listen. They do not bend. They're deaf, not only to charm, threats, and cajoling but also to logic—even when there is good reason to question the data that feeds their conclusions," she writes. Human victims of bad algorithms "are held to a far higher standard of evidence than the algorithms themselves."

But wait, it gets worse. Algorithms can reflect the biases and prejudices of the people who write them. A biased algorithm has no way of knowing that it's biased, which can lead to all kinds of unpleasant outcomes for people applying for everything from car loans to parole from prison.

Skills You Need to Become a Data Scientist

Despite the aura of uncertainty surrounding AI, we are clearly entering an era in which machines are getting smarter and data scientists are rapidly becoming indispensable. If you have data science skills, your prospects look very good.

In 2012, the *Harvard Business Review* published an article with the provocative title, "Data Scientist: Sexiest Job of the 21st Century." The article was widely circulated and cited, setting off a chain reaction of chatter that has yet to fully subside. Follow-up articles in other publications described data scientists as mysterious, powerful, and all-knowing beings who would change the face of business and industry.

What are the skills you need to become a data scientist? The answer depends on whom you ask.

A good data scientist should be familiar with basic statistical principles, advanced statistics, and various types of data, including big data, says Tallapragada. "Data science is still partly art, so you need to develop some intuition, which only comes from experience," he adds.

Drew Conway is the head of data and strategy at Augury, a company that predicts the visual appeal of websites across demographic groups. Way back in 2010, Conway created a Venn diagram depicting the "basic" skills required of a data scientist.

His diagram indicates that math and statistics are important, but they're not the only skills you need to succeed. Thinking creatively and understanding the impact of your work on the outside world are also essential skills for a data scientist.

"Data science is a team sport," says Tian Zheng, a professor of statistics at Columbia University and associate director for education at Columbia's Data Science Institute. "There is a lot of collaboration between data scientists, data engineers, and domain experts. Data scientists bring creativity and insights to such a collaboration, translating a domain question to a data question, exploring and navigating multiple data sources, interpreting trends and patterns found by machine learning algorithms, identifying and addressing limitation of observed data, and decomposing and scoping a data-driven solution for a business/real-world problem into a data science workflow."

From Zheng's perspective, each data science workflow is a sequence of decisions on data sources, feature-engineering procedures, computational infrastructure, algorithms, models, and tools for delivering products. Data scientists are the "humans in the loop" who make these decisions, she says.

It's unlikely the role of data scientist will be automated out of existence anytime soon. That said, the duties and responsibilities of data scientists inevitably will change and evolve over time.

"Currently, data scientists still spend a lot of time and effort on scripting their own machine learning codes and building their own visualizations, often from scratch," Zheng says. "As computational technology develops more data science modules that can streamline some of the most common data science operations, data scientists will become more like designers of pipelines for solving problems."

For the foreseeable future, data scientists will remain the "humans in the loop," she predicts.

AI is Part of the Emerging DARQ Stack

Without overstressing the point, it's clear that data science and AI are transforming many aspects of our lives. But they aren't the only factors in a tsunami of change that's sweeping over global markets. For the past four or five years, technology journalists like me have been writing about the SMAC stack, which stands for social, mobile, analytics, and cloud. Today, we're writing about the DARQ stack, which stands for distributed ledger (DL), artificial intelligence (AI), extended reality (XR), and quantum computing (QC).

Undoubtedly, you will be reading and hearing a lot about the DARQ stack in the years ahead, until it's replaced by a new set of essential technologies. For data scientists, the emergence of the DARQ stack is good news, since it marks the acceptance of AI as a fundamental technology layer that cannot be overlooked or ignored.

The transition of AI from the margins of technology to the mainstream of society is not a trivial occurrence, and all of us have ringside seats at what promises to be a truly game-changing moment in human history.

Yet the DARQ stack is merely the tip of an iceberg. If you really need something to worry about, consider how the next generation of products and services built on the DARQ stack will completely alter our traditional perceptions of reality.

A decade from now, give or take a few years, we'll be using DARQ tech to simulate or fake anything we can imagine. Fake news will be the *least* of our problems. We'll have fake identities, fake pets, fake faces, fake homes, and fake lives. In a world in which our basic notions of reality can be easily manipulated by technology, understanding data science might be the key to sanity and survival.

Meantime, leaders at every level of the organization must become increasingly knowledgeable about tools and solutions for continual learning and development. Today's workforce expects employers to provide opportunities for growth and career development, especially in "hot" fields such as data science and AI.

But you don't have to be a data scientist or an AI savant to see the big picture: organizations that don't provide employees with the tools and capabilities they need to advance their skills continually will be unable to compete successfully in tomorrow's economy.

AI is now inextricably woven into the digital transformation process, and it should be treated as a primary component of every transformational strategy.

AFTERWORD

As a futurist, I spend most of my time listening to people describe what they are most excited about; what they are most apprehensive about; and how they are thinking and/or preparing for what comes after what comes next.

The work of nonfiction you have in your hands will provide you with most of the information you need to successfully guide yourself and your organization through the many pitfalls associated with business transformation.

Historians, anthropologists, and paleo-sociologists will tell you that there are two traits that differentiate *Homo sapiens* from the rest of the biomass:

Trait #1: the ability to contemplate multiple futures, over varying time frames.

Trait #2: the ability to collaborate/cooperate at scale (i.e. share knowledge between tribes and across generations).

The author of this book has one of the most interesting stories and is one of the most gifted storytellers I have met in the last 25 years. A respected thought leader, bordering-on-prescient technologist, and successful senior executive at one of the iconic companies of the day, Yuri Aguiar has distilled thousands of hours of research with companies doing digital transformation right, wrong, and uniquely into an accessible compendium of stories, frameworks, tools, and techniques you can apply to your personal circumstance. To choose not to take advantage of this treasure trove of knowledge borders on malfeasance.

Aristotle—essentially the birth-father of knowledge in the Western canon—always started his path of knowledge creation in a particular field by inventorying and then summarizing a range of endoxa, "the views of fairly reflective people after some reflection." Yuri has interviewed some of the most interesting and noteworthy actors on the global economic stage.

The Chinese have an aphorism, "To know the road ahead, ask those coming back." Yuri has camped out on the road back from successful digital transformation and interviewed most of the survivors.

Yuri is a transformation artist turned scientist. He was an early pioneer in transformation, beginning initiatives before the topic was "discovered" by consultants, academics, journalists, and research analysts. Having extensive hands-on, in-the-trenches, "This-has-to-work-or-there-will-be-career-consequences" digital transformation experience, he is uniquely qualified to synthesize the abundant data now available. He is probably one of the leading thinkers on pragmatic digital transformation.

Data about Digital Transformation

Every organization, *every* executive, *every* individual, and *every* object is on a digital journey. Sadly, most have no map, no compass, and bad shoes (i.e. there is no explicitly stated digital endpoint; there are no metrics to assess how the journey is going; and the gear, skills, competencies, and mindsets required to make the journey are sorely lacking).

Not digitally transforming is simply not an option. Data collected at the Digital Value Institute (tDVI) indicates that less than 10% of companies in the global 2000 believe their current business model will remain economically viable over the next 10 years. Every business leader has to become a digital leader, creating and communicating a vision for one's enterprise.

Boards of directors are pressuring CEOs to "get busy" with digital transformation. Money—big money—is being spent on digital transformation. In the early stages of GE's digital transformation, my fraternity brother at Dartmouth College, CEO Jeffrey Immelt, invested over $200 billion in digital initiatives. In 2019 global investment in digital transformation initiatives is expected to reach $2.2 trillion (~$1.3 trillion was spent in 2018).

There are big benefits to successfully digitally transforming your enterprise. Subscription research firms forecast that digital transformation will generate $18 trillion in added business value (IDC) and generate 36% of overall revenue by 2020

(Gartner). Digital transformation initiatives have stock price impact. Digital Value Institute research indicates that a subset of the 3% of the publicly traded general business population who successfully transformed achieved a 300% stock price increase.

Truth be told, CEOs don't really care about the particular technologies that enable digital transformation (i.e. analytics, artificial intelligence, augmented/virtual reality, big data, blockchain, cloud, machine learning, Internet of Things/IoT, robotics, search engine optimization/SEO, 3D/4D printing, voice-friendly apps, and/or wearables). They care about the benefits (e.g. stock price increase, market share expansion, cost structure reduction, risk minimization/improved risk management) digital transformation enables.

Few companies are achieving the results envisioned. Surveys and interviews indicate that only 14% of the companies attempting to digitally transform have been able to generate "substantive improvements in business results." Many organizations are frustrated with the lack of results and pace of digital transformation they are experiencing. The consensus of analysts is that a third of organizations attempting digital transformation will fail at it.

Catastrophic failure to achieve digital transformation can result in organizations becoming symbols/icons of ineptitude:

"Kodak-ed" (i.e. failing to jump to the next technological wave);

"Netflix-ed" (i.e. failing to adapt to changing customer buying patterns);

"Amazon-ed" (i.e. having digital competitors render product/services irrelevant);

"Tesla-ed" (i.e. having charismatic outsiders co-opt critical destination points on digital horizon);

"Uber-ed" (i.e. offering subpar customer experiences); and most recently,

"AI-ed" (i.e. having algorithmic competitors outsmart incumbent offerings).

Everything possible today was at one time impossible. Everything impossible today may at some time in the future be possible. The future is not something that just happens to us.

The future is something we create. Digital transformation is how we create the future.

Digital competence/digital maturity level is being measured. The Fletcher School at Tufts has created—on a nation-state level—a metric for measuring a political entity's digital maturity (The Digital Evolution Index or DEI). The metric parses nation-states into four digital categories:

1. Stall Out: countries which are losing momentum and falling behind.

2. Stand Out: countries showing high levels of digital development.

3. Watch Out: countries facing both significant opportunities and challenges.

4. Break Out: countries having the potential to develop strong digital economies.

Most digital transformations are inwardly focused on improving existing business processes—not on launching new products or services or interacting with external partners through digital channels. Domino's Pizza Inc. has embraced digital, emphasizing all the ways you can order pizza with minimal human and maximal digital contact. It's introduced myriad ordering modalities—Facebook, Twitter, Twitter with emojis, Apple Watch, voice-activated, and "zero click."

Customers can track their pizzas online, starting from as they're being made all the way to delivery. Digital has been good for Domino's. Since the end of 2008, its share price has increased sixtyfold. Domino's went from having a 9% share of the pizza restaurant market in 2009 to 15% in 2016.[1] They deliver over a million pizzas a day. Four-fifths of Domino's sales come through digital channels.

The time to perform a digital transformation is *now*. Ninety percent of the global 10,000 have embarked on at least one "digital experiment." Eight-five percent of enterprise decision-makers believe they have two years to integrate digital initiatives before falling behind their competitors.

---

[1] https://www.bloomberg.com/opinion/articles/2016-12-27/domino-s-delivery-tech-goes-from-dial-up-to-drones.

Fifty-five percent of companies think they only have one year. Organizations need to realize while they must start now, the transformation journey is a lengthy one (a marathon, not a sprint). Four out of five executives say their organization will be a digital business within three years.

Every successful digital transformation made information more available inside and outside the organization. Finland has gone so far as to pass a law stating that Internet access is a birthright.

Many digital transformations gave the customer significant voice in product and service design.

Every successful digital transformation created and managed a clear change narrative (description of, case for, and feedback regarding the changes being made). In many instances, these narratives included compelling "anchor visuals" (pictures that helped explain things). Cognitive scientists tell us that visuals communicate information to the brain 60,000 times faster than text.

IT can become an obstacle to digital transformation. Legacy systems do not support—were not initially designed for—the nearly instant, free, and precise ability to connect people, devices, and physical objects anywhere. Without optimizing how IT itself operates within a company, efforts to improve internal and external systems and processes with cloud computing, artificial intelligence, automation, and other capabilities risk hitting a bottleneck that leaves the entire business lagging behind competitors. Less than 20% of business leaders feel like they have the right technology in place.

Digital transformation requires executives outside of technology becoming comfortable with technology. A survey conducted by the MIT Center for Information Systems Research showed that out of 1,233 publicly traded companies with revenues over $1 billion only 24% had board members who were classified as technology experts. A 2018 HBR survey asked 5,000 board members around the world what activities they thought their boards were good at. Technology and innovation ranked 17th and 18th. A variety of comfort-expanding methods including technology petting zoos and curated board member roadtrips to technology conferences have been experimented with.

Traditional processes of direction setting, resource allocation, and systems/capabilities building are no longer sufficient. The conventional, linear, and time-consuming "wait-and-respond" approach to strategy—where plans are created and finalized in a staff portion of the enterprise, subsequently distributed for comment to the IT department, and then pushed through an industrial-age procurement process—are out-of-step with the pace of modern business.

During a digital transformation, incumbent companies may need to upgrade the digital skills of the enterprise. A variety of techniques have been deployed:

- Reverse mentoring (younger, digitally savvy employees coach more seasoned executives).

- Company-wide training programs (with bespoke uplift curricula).

- Digital certification programs.

Tools and Techniques

Honest Assessment

What is being measured? Where is money *really* being spent—running the business (activities necessary to compete in current markets), growing the business, or transforming the business (changing how we operate/changing how the industry operates)?

- Percentage of budget being spent maintaining systems of record.

- Percentage of budget being spent maintaining systems of engagement.

- Percentage of resources and budget allocated to identifying, testing, and validating new technologies.

- Percentage of resources and budget allocated to new businesses or acquisitions.

- Inventory of skills and capabilities (gap analysis—what you have and what you need).

- Percentage of revenue generated by digital products/services.

- Number of innovation ideas generated.

- Number of innovation ideas that resulted in new products/services.

- Time to move from ideas to prototype to market.

Competence in four foundational digital areas:

1. Data analytics
2. Privacy and security management
3. Digital roadmapping
4. Results tracking

A big mistake made by many organizations during a digital transformation is to measure activities, not outcomes. For example, call centers should measure the percentage of customer problems solved, not how quickly they ended the call. A robust and rapidly evolving set of metrics are available to guide transformation efforts:

- KPIs (Key Performance Indicators)

- OKRs (Objectives and Key Results)

- ROIs (Returns on Investment)

- NPSs (Net Promoter Score—management tool used to gauge the loyalty of a firm's customer relationships)

Industrial-age macro-measurements are probably not giving us the right big-picture view of the transformation landscape. How do you measure the value of the increasing amount of free goods available online, including Wikipedia articles, Google maps, Facebook interactions, smartphone apps, and YouTube videos?

Shared Vision

Digital transformation requires a shared vision. Fumbled transformation efforts can seem like the Indian parable of the five blind men and the elephant (where each tribe in the organization feels a different part of the animal and comes away with a totally different picture of the beast). You can't ask the IT guy, "What is digital transformation?" and have him/her geek out about the latest in machine learning and cloud portability. Neither can you have the operations person perceive digital transformation as just being about a 1-click customer experience. If the line-of-business person only thinks in terms of business model change (e.g. moving from product sale to services), you will have problems.

The economist John Maynard Keynes reminds us, "The real difficulty in changing any enterprise lies not in developing new ideas, but in escaping from the old ones." As a coxswain at Dartmouth I learned that it is much easier to have everyone row harder when there is a shared vision of where the finish line is.

A Managed Transformation Process

There are many aspects to a digital transformation (e.g. knowledge/vision, persuasion, decision, implementation/

information security and confirmation/communication). Each has to be measured and managed.

Having a few digital initiatives underway does not constitute a digital strategy. Yuri has created a simple five-step process called "SMART Transformation Process":

S Strategy

M Mapping

A Alignment

R Research

T Transform

Customer Experience

Organizations need to map out the exact steps customers go through when engaging with your business. With this customer journey map completed, one can launch a discovery process aimed at identifying which emerging technologies will enhance key touchpoints in their journey.

Many organizations have stalled at what I call the "simple digital" phase of digital transformation. They have used the rich set of technologies available to improve how the organization interacts with customers. This is great, but this is not the endpoint of digital transformation.

Organizational messages have to be personalized. The term of art currently being bandied about is *hyperpersonalized*.

This is not about the company. It has to be about the customer. Consumers increasingly expect their world to be "smart" and seamlessly adapt to their taste and habits.

Consumers at the front-edge are evolving—while digital natives ask what they can do with technology, data natives are more concerned about what technology can autonomously do for them. Digital natives use the Starbucks mobile app. Data natives want the app to know their favorite drinks—and when to suggest a new one.

We are migrating beyond our current parent-to-child relationship with technology where we need to tell it what to do very specifically and correct often.

Employee Experience

The objective is to ensure that employees willingly and effectively embrace relevant, high-impact technology, rather than feel threatened by it. One has to authentically deal with concern/fear regarding job loss associated with digital transformation initiatives.

Data about Data

Michael Porter, an economist and researcher who teaches at Harvard Business School, observes that most workers today are simply overwhelmed by data: "The machines are smart and connected, but the people are just sitting out there wondering what's going on." Is there someone in the enterprise thinking about how key constituencies (both internal and external to the enterprise) think about data?

Everything generates data. The question is—are you getting full value from that data stream? GE CEO Immelt once observed, "A locomotive today is a rolling data center." Data boffins lament that in 2018 only 1% of the data generated was effectively utilized. They expect this to rise to 3–4% by 2020. Thirty percent of large enterprises are expected to commence generating Data-as-a-Service revenue by 2020.

To enable future experiences that exceed customer expectations will require being able to digitally identify the customer, and allow the customer to own, understand, consent to, and share their data. Some organizations have gone so far as to encourage/enable customers to create and manage their own data sets regarding the relationship with the enterprise.

Data within the enterprise has to be cleansed, de-siloed, and shared.

Structural Accommodations

Many organizations (~60%) have created new business units/ new executive positions specifically dedicated to digital. Spanish bank Banco Bilbao Vizcaya Argentaria SA established a separate legal entity several years ago dedicated to data science.

Some organizations have created new digital roles (e.g. chief digital officer). Less than 25% of large global enterprises have appointed chief digital officers, chief data officers, or digital ambassadors—Barclays has created a "Digital Eagles" designation for transformation evangelists.

Digital Identity

In a simpler time (the eighteenth, nineteenth, and twentieth centuries) food was a universal identifier. Jean Anthelme Brillat-Savarin summed this up with, *Si tu me dis ce que tu manges, je peux te dire qui tu es* ("If you tell me what you eat, I can tell you who you are").

Today how you interact with information (e.g. the technologies you use, how and to what purposes you use them) defines who you are. Sheryl Connelly, a friend who is a futurist at Ford Motor Company, believes, "Since the Great Recession, status is not found in stuff. Status is having information."

In 1993 Peter Steiner created a cartoon with the caption "On the Internet nobody knows you're a dog." In 2020 and beyond, such anonymity is impossible. Today we all live in a digital glass house. A fellow futurist interpreted this as implying, "Since we are all naked, we might as well be buff." I think what he means by this is that because how we interact with information is so transparent and essentially defines us, we might as well be aware of and proud of our digital behaviors.

My former boss, ur-Futurist Alvin Toffler, forecast: "The illiterate of the 21st century will not be those who cannot read and write, but those who cannot learn, unlearn, and relearn." Reading this book will accelerate you and your organization down the digital transformation learning curve.

Thornton May

Futurist, author of *The New Know:*

Innovation Powered by Analytics

ABOUT THE AUTHOR

Yuri Aguiar is the chief innovation and transformation officer at the Ogilvy Group. Prior to that he was the strategic portfolio director at the global technology unit supporting companies within the WPP Group.

He has been a CIO, CTO, and director of worldwide technology operations over his career as a global leader in business technology. He prides himself in leading small efficient teams of independent thinkers who challenge the status quo.

Yuri recently completed his Masters in Digital Marketing to better understand challenges around consumer data. His thesis, *The Evolution of Consumer and Marketer Responses to Technology Enabled Marketing*, studied consumer habits across multiple social media channels, geographies, and demographics. His most recent undertaking has been the design and testing of the SMART Digital Transformation© process in order to create a simple narrative between digital proficiency and technical proficiency. He is currently pursuing interests in the data science area with experiments in advanced content intelligence while working on a patent around augmented reality.

He also pursues inspiration through hobbies that find expression outside of work. An avid music and aviation fan, he loves spending downtime on a flight simulator. Yuri has partnered with colleagues to organize charity concerts for Breast Cancer, U.S. Veterans, and for victims of the tsunami in Japan—often performing with the band.

A hands-on leader with experience working across three countries and interacting with countries on every continent, Yuri has written this book with the intent of sharing his own work experiences and lessons learned from very intelligent people along the course of his career thus far. And a testament, he hopes, for his own business motto: "Good execution is the key to a great strategy."

INDEX

227